Amy's Wish

A Romantic Comedy by

Tom Sharkey

SAMUEL FRENCH, INC.

45 West 25th Street   7623 Sunset Boulevard
NEW YORK 10010   HOLLYWOOD 90046
LONDON   *TORONTO*

ISBN 0 573 63000 3   Printed in U.S.A.   #2999

IMPORTANT BILLING AND CREDIT REQUIREMENTS

All producers of AMY'S WISH *must* give credit to the Author of the Play in all programs distributed in connection with performances of the Play and in all instances in which the title of the Play appears for purposes of advertising, publicizing or otherwise exploiting the Play and/or a production. The name of the Author *must* appear on a separate line on which no other name appears, immediately following the title, and *must* appear in size of type not less than fifty percent the size of the title type.

CAST OF CHARACTERS

SAM GALWAY, a retired newspaper reporter who marries—

AMY GALWAY, an ingenuous old dear who wishes she again was—

SCOOTER GALWAY, a nineteen-year-old knockout who captivates—

JEFF CRENSHAW, a young romantic who hopes to save her from—

HOWARD MONTEITH, a suspicious sheriff who has been alerted by—

IRMA PRY, a nosy neighbor who just *knows* Sam did the old girl in.

TIME:
The present.

PLACE:
A studio-condo in Fountain Springs, Florida.

ACT I
Scene 1: Late on a rainy evening.
Scene 2: The following morning.
Scene 3: That evening.

ACT II
Scene 1: Later that evening.
Scene 2: An instant later.
Scene 3: Early the next morning.

For Felicia - Always

ACT I

Scene 1

(After houselights fall, there is organ music: the ad lib, unobtrusive sort played before a wedding—or perhaps during a wake. In the dark we hear:)

SAM GALWAY. I was a man of the world— *(Spot hits him *d.l.; hard on some edges, soft on many others, he is a comfortably likable senior who wears a rose in the lapel of his best dark suit and addresses us in a reflective mood.)* —a retired newspaper reporter.

AMY GALWAY. *(Still in the dark.)* I was a woman of the world— *(Another spot hits her d.r.; an endearingly ingenuous senior whose edges are all soft, she wears a corsage on her best dress, which is predominantly white, and the hint of a white veil as she also addresses us.)* —a retired cook—waitress—typist—cook again— *(Proudly.)* and chief nutritionist for General Foods.

SAM. *(After a beat.)* Then I went to the wrong Holiday Inn in Kenosha and barged into a Gray Panthers rally.

AMY. Then I went to the *right* Holiday Inn in Kenosha and my Wednesday night Gray Panthers rally.

SAM. I had fallen in love only once.

AMY. *I* had fallen in love only once.

SAM. *(Didn't know this, doesn't like it, addresses her directly:)* Oh yeah?

AMY. *(A plea for understanding.)* I was nineteen, Sam! There

*NOTE: For purposes of clarity, all l. and r. directions are from the audience's point of view.

are few things more passionate than a nineteen-year-old girl! *(To us, brightly.)* Walford was a baseball player.

SAM. *(Can't believe it.)* Walford?

AMY. *(Insists to him.)* Yes! *(To us.)* He moved down to St. Louis hoping to become a Cardinal.

SAM. *(Curious.)* Did he make it—?

AMY. *(To him.)* No. *(To us, sad—though happy enough for Walford.)* But he did become a parish priest.

SAM. *(Relief.)* Ohhh. *(To us, the reflective mood restored.)* The girl I fell in love with also was nineteen.

AMY. *(Does not like this at all, to him.) Nineteen?*

SAM. *(Continues to us as if he didn't hear her.)* I was fourteen.

AMY. *(Has to laugh.)* Oh, Sam!

SAM. *(To her, insists.)* There is *nothing* more passionate than a fourteen-year-old boy! *(To us.)* Miss Quimby was my homeroom teacher.

AMY. *(To him.)* Quimby?

SAM. *(To her.)* Better than Walford! *(To us.)* I thought she was perfect.

AMY. *(To us.)* I thought Walford was perfect.

SAM. *(To us, sadly.)* But when it didn't work out—

AMY. *(To us, just as sadly.)* But when we didn't work out—

SAM. I knew I'd have to wait till I found someone I could love as much or more.

AMY. I knew I'd have to wait till I found someone I could love as much—or more. *(Turns to face him, caring awfully.)* And I never did, Sam!—

SAM. *(Cares so much it hurts.)* I didn't either, Amy!—

(Music pauses.)

AMY. Until you.
SAM. Until you.

(Music explodes into the climactic final fifteen notes of the Lohengrin Wedding March and they meet d.c., his hands on her shoulders, her hands on his arms, and pore into each other's eyes; lights fade to black and we hear the sound of rain.)

JEFF CRENSHAW. *(In the dark.)* Welcome to sunny Florida, folks! Is it true you just got married? *(An attempt to get their attention:)* Mr. and Mrs. Galway! Were you married only this afternoon?

(Lights up on a studio-condo; furnishings include an open sofa-bed with pillows, sheets and blanket, two easy chairs, two end tables with lamps; a wall phone and a u.s.-facing TV; an open door l. leads to a porch; a doorway u.l. leads to the kitchen; u.c. is a wide closet with sliding doors; u.r. is the bathroom door; JEFF, a tall, clean-cut young man, is in the act of setting down two suitcases; he wears an open rubber slicker over white slacks and a white tee shirt with a motto printed across its chest and a pen stuck in its collar; SAM and AMY have raincoats draped over their shoulders and three more suitcases at their feet—one a jonquil yellow—but are otherwise exactly as we saw them last: still standing d.c. and poring into each other eyes.)

JEFF. *(Another attempt.)* Mr. and Mrs. Gal—

HOWARD. *(Off.)* Oh, let them be, Jeff! *(HOWARD MONTEITH appears in porch doorway; a big, friendly bear of a man of about SAM's age, he wears a Stetson, star, pistol and handcuffs, and is closing a black umbrella that he leaves outside on entering; with a fond look at the entranced couple:)* They're answering your question.

JEFF. *(Acknowledges him.)* Oh hi, Sheriff Monteith.

SAM. *(Head jerks up.)* Monteith, did you say? *(Turns around and sees him.)* Howard! *(Drops his coat on bed and goes to him.)* You son of a gun!

HOWARD. *(As they heartily shake hands.)* You ink-stained yellow journalist!

SAM. You flatulent old—

HOWARD. *(Stops the hand-shaking with a stern:)* Careful. *(Both men laugh and he indicates AMY, who is observing them, having also dropped her coat on bed.)* So this is *her?*

SAM. Who? *(Remembering his bride.)* Oh! Amy! Honey, I want you to meet—

AMY. *(Gently interrupts.)* I don't believe an introduction's necessary. *(Takes HOWARD's hand.)* Howard Monteith! I feel I already know you. Sam told me how you two used to jump into your squad car and chase the bad guys in Milwaukee—you in the line of duty, Sam in a cold sweat. *(As HOWARD glances in his direction, SAM embarrassedly acknowledges this truth.)* You're one of the main reasons we moved to Fountain Springs.

HOWARD. *(Feigns surprise.)* Not so old Sam could try the Fountain of Youth?

SAM. *(Would warn him off.)* Howard—

AMY. *(Does not understand.)* The Fountain of Youth!?

JEFF. *(Always helpful.)* That's what our retirement community's named for, ma'am. *(Opens slicker wide.)* See what my tee shirt says?

AMY. *(Would like to, but:)* Not without my glasses.

JEFF. *(Runs a finger along the motto.)* "Grow Young with Me at Fountain Springs—Where the Best is Yet to Be!"

AMY. *(Charmed.)* Oh my.

HOWARD. *(Amplifies.)* A night like this, a real storm out there— *(Lights blink as we hear the sizzle of lightning and a thunderclap.)*— see what I mean?—water rushes underground from all the hills around us, creating the thousands of fountains Ponce de Leon checked out. Course, he never found the one he was looking for....

AMY. *(Terribly curious.)* But could it be—it's really out there? *Can* people grow young again?

HOWARD. *(Laughs.)* That's what I was kidding Sam about! See, I thought a sip might help him some. *(As she regards him blankly, confides sotto voce.)* This being his wedding night.

SAM. *(Embarrassed.)* Howard—!

(But AMY interrupts with a cry so sad that it might break your heart.)

AMY. Ooooooh! Ooooooh! *(Then the saddest word she knows:)* Gee-ma-*net*-ly!!!

(After a quick look around through teary eyes for somewhere to retreat to, rushes into bathroom, closing door.)

JEFF. *(As upset as any one of them, demands.)* What did you say, Sheriff?
HOWARD. *(To SAM.)* What did I say?
JEFF. *(Confused.)* That's what *I* said. What did he say?
SAM. *(A calming influence.)* It's all right, it's all right. She's been doing this all day. *(Takes out a pocket notebook.)* See, I made some notes and— *(Unable to find a pen, removes the one clipped to JEFF's shirt.)* Borrow this?
JEFF. *(Being as the pen's already gone.)* Oh sure.

(Needing an excuse to stay and listen, busies himself by lining up the suitcases.)

SAM. *(Perplexed as he turns pages, trying to find the notes:)* First she's up … then she's down … then she's—
AMY. *(Off, calls gently.)* Sa-am!
HOWARD. *(Dares to hope.)* Up again?
SAM. *(Uncertain.)* Maybe. (At the door.) Yes, dear?
AMY. *(Off.)* I need—well, I need my—

(Continues to speak but the rest is in a voice so low that SAM has to put his head against the door to listen; JEFF, who would like to listen too, leans in.)

HOWARD. *(Curtly.)* Jeff—!
JEFF. *(Protests.)* But she's such a sweet old lady! I thought

maybe I could help.

    HOWARD. Don't you have more luggage to bring in?

    JEFF. Oh, just a big old trunk.

    HOWARD. *(With authority.)* Get it.

(More LIGHTNING and THUNDER as an unhappy JEFF pulls slicker tight about him and exits.)

    HOWARD. *(On seeing SAM has turned away from door.)* So where is she, up or down?

    SAM. I'm not exactly sure … but she says she needs her jonquil suitcase.

    HOWARD. *(Solemn.)* "Jonquil," ha?

(Both men look at the suitcases, obviously with no idea what "jonquil" means; but since all but one are black, that one being yellow; SAM finally points at it.)

    SAM. That's it.

    HOWARD. Gotta be.

    SAM. *(At the door with suitcase.)* Amy?

(She puts a hand out without a word and takes the suitcase, closing door.)

    HOWARD. *(A shrewd observation.)* Could be—maybe—she's somewhere in the middle.

    SAM. *(More upset than he'd like to show.)* Who *knows,* Howard? See, these notes I made…. *(Back in the book.)* She was okay all through the ceremony *and* on the plane ride—except once when I mentioned *(Finds the note.)* what a beautiful "bride" she was.

    HOWARD. *(Listening attentively.)* Huh.

    SAM. And then when I said how lucky we were at our ages *(Another note.)* to be going on a "honeymoon."

HOWARD. *(Trying to fit the clue in.)* I see.

SAM. And then when I said—

HOWARD. You sure said a lot, Sam.

SAM. Yeah— *(Reading.)* —we were bound to have some "great new *experiences*" here. *(Another note.)* Oh! And when I wondered how comfortable we'd be—at least till we found a bigger place—sharing a "sofa-bed."

HOWARD. *(Frowning in concentration.) Hmm.* So what'd she say when you said these things?

SAM. You know. *(A poor imitation.)* "Geemanetly!"

HOWARD. Huh!

SAM. But then she was fine again—at least I thought she was—until *you* mentioned— *(Writing it.)* —"wedding night."

HOWARD. By golly—!

(Stumped as to an explanation, HOWARD removes his hat to scratch his head.)

SAM. *(Also stumped, reading notes.)* "Bride" ... "honeymoon" ... "great new experiences"—

HOWARD. *(Reading over SAM's shoulder.)* "Sofa-bed"—

SAM. "Wedding night." What could all these things possibly have in common???

HOWARD. *(Still stumped.)* Huh! *(Then:) Huhhh.*

SAM. *(On meeting HOWARD's eyes.)* But that *can't* be it! She was a woman of the world, she said—a waitress, typist, cook—two times!—and chief nutritionist for General Foods.

JEFF. *(As he carries in a monster of a wooden trunk.)* Well, this is the last of it. You're about all set.

SAM. *(Staring at notes.)* Naw, *can't* be.

JEFF. *(Brightly.)* Oh *sure* you are! New sheets, new pillow cases, all the electricity and plumbing working—which is pretty good, considering this is a brand new wing and they just put your well in. *(Beat, his main concern:)* Now as for that woman in the bathroom—

HOWARD. *(Who has to duck as JEFF takes a step toward bathroom with the big, unwieldy trunk.)* Jeff! Just put the trunk down, ha?

JEFF. *(Happy to oblige.)* Where? *(A step toward closet.)* In here?

SAM. *(Still in his notes.)* No!

JEFF. *(Misunderstanding, suggests a place against the wall.)* OK—over here?

SAM. *(As above.)* For Pete's sake—no!

JEFF. *(Stops, still misunderstanding.)* Would you give me a little hint, sir?

HOWARD. *(Patience gone.)* Here, Jeff! Right *here! (Helps him set the obviously heavy trunk down next to the TV and walks him to the door.)* Now go home and see your folks—and don't you show your face around here till the brunch tomorrow.

JEFF. *(Missing his tip.)* You mean … that's it?

SAM. *(A near explosion.)* Ye gods—it just *can't* be!

JEFF. *(Relief.)* I was *hoping* you might say that, sir.

SAM. *(Having looked up on this last, regards JEFF in confusion.)* Are you addressing me, young man?

HOWARD. *(Politely guiding JEFF out door.)* Jeff was just, uh, leaving.

SAM. No! Wait! *(Starts across to JEFF, digging in his pockets.)* I have something for you.

JEFF. That's good to hear and, let me say, I do appreciate—

SAM. Thanks a lot *(Returns the pen and closes door on JEFF; on turning to HOWARD.)* Howard, there is just no way! She's been sending me signals ever since I met her!

HOWARD. *(As he considers this.)* Before we were married, my Mavis sent *me* signals … then I learned they were in code. *(A sudden frown.)* Speaking of whom— *(Checks watch.)* Uh oh, she'll be waiting. *(Restores his hat and adds:)* For what I've never figured out.

SAM. *(Near desperation.)* You're not leaving *too?*

HOWARD. Hey, it's late, Sam— *(Reminds him.)* and you're a married man.

SAM. *(Unhappy.)* Well, I sure don't feel like one.

HOWARD. Your wife's upset, you don't know why—and are afraid to ask her, right?

SAM. Yeah....

HOWARD. You feel like a married man. You're just not used to it. *(Opens door.)* Have a nice evening, hear?

SAM. *(In pain.)* Howard!

HOWARD. *(Who regretted the automatic words as soon as they were uttered.)* Sorry.

(HOWARD exits, closing door.)

SAM. *(Disgusted with his life.)* "Have a nice evening!" Ha! *(More lightning and thunder; implores the heavens.)* Why would any sensible person build *two* Holiday Inns in Kenosha???

AMY. *(Off, in a voice so gentle it's alluring.)* Sa-am, did that nice boy leave?

SAM. Jeff? Yeah, Howard sent him home.

AMY. *(Off.)* Then Howard is still here?

SAM. No, hon, he's gone too.

AMY. *(Off.)* Then you and I are—totally alone?

SAM. *(Not knowing what to think.)* So...?

(AMY enters joyously, looking lovelier than ever in a robe and negligee, her hair perhaps let down.)

AMY. So I'm ready whenever you are!

SAM. *(As he stares in awe.)* For what?

AMY. *(Pouts.)* Why ... whatever's customary.

SAM. *(Accusingly.)* You *know* what's customary!

AMY. Of course I do! *(With some trepidation.)* Don't you?

SAM. *(A quick glance at notebook.)* I was right! No, I was wrong! *(Beat.)* I am so confused!

AMY. What is it, Sam? My negligee? What I've done to my

hair? They haven't installed the bathroom mirror yet—is it my makeup?

SAM. No, no, no, you're beautiful. I just thought when you were crying—well, see, I've got these clues here. *(With the notebook.)* "Bride, honeymoon, great new experiences, sofa-bed," and "wedding night." When I said them—when you heard them— *(Sets notebook, still open, on r. end table.)* Why'd they set you off?

AMY. *(Though at first it seems she is about to cry again—)* Ooooooh— *(It is the entry into laughter.)* Ho! Ho! *(Loving him for his concern.)* I guess I got a little silly, Sam—but many a new bride is!

SAM. *(Dares to hope.)* Then—you mean—you're *not* afraid— of what might happen *now?*

AMY. Oh, how *could* I be? *(Goes to him.)* Sam Galway, you're the kindest, sweetest, dearest man I've ever met—!

SAM. *(Pleased but bashful.)* You really mean that, huh?

AMY. Of course I do, my darling! *(As if just now noticing.)* But aren't you just a little warm in that jacket? And that shirt and tie?

(She begins to loosen his tie for him.)

SAM. Yeah, and getting warmer by the minute. *(Beat.)* I'll change in here.

(He exits into bathroom.)

AMY. *(Would point the suitcase out.)* The—
SAM. *(Off.)* Jonquil suitcase! Got it.

(He closes door.)

AMY. You see, those words—those "clues," as you say— brought back memories of Walford.

SAM. *(Head immediately out door.)* Him again?
AMY. Not in that way!… Honest!

SAM. *(A beat—then solemnly:)* Okay.

(He closes door.)

AMY. How can I explain? Marrying you today—well, it just did not seem fair, that's all.

SAM. *(Head out door again.)* To *Walford?*

AMY. Will you stop popping out like Pop-Tarts? It didn't seem fair to *you!*

SAM. *(Again a beat and solemnly:)* Okay.

(He closes door again.)

AMY. *(Who throughout the next few lines will move three of the suitcases into the closet, set the fourth beside the bed, turn back the blanket and a sheet and, after trying to slide the trunk aside, decide—it is so heavy!—to leave it where it is.)* What I'm saying is, I thought I'd really loved the man—just as you'd loved—

SAM. *(Off, supplies the name.)* Miss Quimby.

AMY. Yes! So I began to wonder: How is it fair that what I had for *him*—if I ever *gave* to him—which I didn't!—though I might have—if he'd asked, I mean—which, darn!, he'd better not have....

SAM. *(Off.)* Are you talking to you or me?

AMY. *Sorry!* All I'm saying is: How is it fair that, having at last found the man I *really* want to give my all to, I no longer really have all that all to give?!

SAM. *(Off.)* But you *do,* sweetheart!

AMY. I *don't!* And that's why I was sad! In fact, it wasn't till just a minute ago that the sadness seemed to go for good!

SAM. *(Off, confused.)* What happened *a minute ago?*

AMY. If I tell you, will you laugh?

SAM. *(Off.)* If I laugh, will you cry again?

AMY. I *might.*

SAM. *(Off.)* I won't laugh.

AMY. Well, just before I came back out, I said a quick prayer to St. Dymphna.

SAM. *(Off.) Who?*

AMY. St. Dymphna! She's an Irish saint—the patron saint of brides. If a bride asks her for something on her wedding night, she gets it—guaranteed.

SAM. *(Off, doubtful.)* Who would guarantee a thing like that?

AMY. *(Apologetically defensive.)* My mother.

SAM. *(Off, astonishment.)* Your *mother? How?* Did she get what *she* wanted on her wedding night?

AMY. Oh, very much so, yes.

SAM. *(Off.)* Through St. Dymphna?

AMY. Not exactly. *(Beat.)* My dad kept her so busy she forgot to pray.

SAM. *(Off, strangulated.)* I ... see.

AMY. You're not laughing, are you?

SAM. *(Off.)* That was a cough, dear. Something in my throat.

AMY. *(Reassured, turns l. lamp off—lights dim slightly—and slips into bed.)* Anyhow, I prayed—for you, Sam—

SAM. *(Reenters, looking his best in pajamas, robe and slippers, doesn't understand.)* You say you prayed for *me?*

AMY. *(Impressed.)* Oh, you look so handsome!

SAM. I always try to on my wedding night.

(He would turn off r. lamp.)

AMY. Wait! *(He leaves it on.)* I prayed not *for* you—but for *you* that I would be—well, just as I was the first time I fell in love.

SAM. *(Likes her.)* A little crazy, you mean.

AMY. *(Likes him.)* That too maybe—but just as I was—exactly! So that what I was for him, my first love, I'd be for you—my great love!

SAM. You mean you actually took the time of a saint to ask for a thing like that?

AMY. But don't you see? It may be working! For as soon as I said the prayer, I started to giggle—and as soon as I giggled, I felt *so* much better!

SAM. *(With some concern.)* Oscar Wilde said, "Be careful what you pray for, it might come true."

AMY. Isn't that: "Be careful what you *wish* for"? *(A thought.)* And was it Oscar Wilde?

SAM. You're right, it was the Pope—and he said, "Be careful what you wish for to St. Dymphna."

AMY. *(Chiding.)* Sam!

SAM. *(With an idea.)* Wait one second.

(He exits into bathroom, leaving the door open.)   ·

AMY. *(As she waits.)* What are you doing in there?

SAM. *(Off.)* I have to ask you, Amy ... did you drink any of this water?

AMY. No...

SAM. *(Returns with a glass of water.)* Okay ... try some.

AMY. *(Reluctant.)* Why?

SAM. Just a sip? For me?

AMY. *(Tries it—and is glad she did.)* Mmm! That's *fresh.*

SAM. Now do you know what you've just done? You've enlisted not only the aid of St. Dymphna and your mother's guarantee but water from a brand new well—maybe the very water Ponce de Leon couldn't find—or, if he found, didn't know how to use because he wasn't an Irish bride and had never heard about St. Dymphna!

AMY. *(Pouts.)* Sam, you're making fun of me.

SAM. *(Tender, sits beside her.)* I'm not, Amy—I swear! See, there's no question that any minute now— *(Sound of rain stops.)* There! It's starting.

AMY. *(Moves away from him, suspicious.)* What is?

SAM. For one thing, the rain's let up.

AMY. *(Hears the "silence," half-impressed.)* It *has.*

SAM. And for another…. *(Goes to l. side of the bed; she moves away from him again.)* Ah, you may elude me, but not your fate! *(Returns to r.)* Darn, if we only had a mirror, I could show you!

AMY. *(Though having started to move away again, stops in curiosity.)* What?

SAM. *(Again sits beside her; this time she does not move.)* Right before my eyes, pet, you are becoming the most beautiful … *(Kisses her hand.)* scrumptu-ous … *(Kisses her other hand.)* and desirable woman … *(Kisses her forehead.)* that I've seen since church today— *(Admits.)* when I said a prayer or two myself.

AMY. It isn't nice to joke about prayer, Sam.

SAM. You're the one who giggled.

AMY. *(Holds him in confusion.)* But I'm not giggling now! Oh, my darling husband! If —if only it were possible for St. Dymphna to do this thing—I so wish she would! I want more than anything to be— *(Beat.)* just to be—!

SAM. *(Never more tender.)* That's my whole point, Amy. She has. And you are.

(He clicks lamp off. Blackout.)

Scene 2

(In the dark we hear the amplified jangle of a mechanical alarm clock. Lights rise on the next morning, allowing us to find SAM'S BRIDE tucked in a corner of the bed, swathed in a sheet and blanket, and SAM some distance from her, clad only in pajamas, flat on his back, spread-eagled and snoring peacefully. The jangle persists until we are sure that one or the other must awaken. But not until it stops and a relatively quiet rooster crows

does SAM sit up and say:)

SAM. What the hell was *that?! (Looks about, sees his bride and because he is still only half-awake:)* Who—? *(Then realizes.)* Oh. *(And then:)* Ohhh. *(This last is accompanied by the warm smile of memory; it's been quite a night.)*

SAM'S BRIDE. *(Who remains beneath the sheet.)* I'm up, Sam.

SAM. *(Playful.)* For what?

SAM'S BRIDE. Don't we have a brunch to go to?

SAM. Can't we order in?

SAM'S BRIDE. *(A bit concerned about him.)* Are you all right, dear?

SAM. *(A happy realization:)* The best I've ever been! *(Intent on preparing for the day, puts on slippers, rises and, not bothering with the robe, picks up the suitcase AMY set beside the bed.)* How about you?

(He exits into bathroom.)

SAM'S BRIDE. *(Sits up, stretches and the sheet falls away to reveal she now wears only the negligee and a smile as warm as SAM's.)* Simply terrific!

(She looks terrific too; AMY EILEEN "SCOOTER" HALLORAN HOLLY is an absolute knockout—and nineteen years of age.)

SAM. *(Off.)* You sure *sound* good.

SCOOTER. It must be the warmer climate. *(Blinks in the light.)* And now that the sun is out—I think my cold is gone.

SAM. *(Off.)* I didn't know you *had* one.

SCOOTER. *(A hand to her throat, surprised.)* Neither did I. *(Notices the back of the hand, checks the other too.)* Well, isn't *that* strange! After all this time!

SAM. *(Off.)* What's that, hon?

SCOOTER. My Porcelana's started working!

SAM *(Off.)* Hmm.

SCOOTER. *(Notices open notebook SAM left on r. end table; frowns and picks it up to read:)* "Bride ... honeymoon ... great new—" *(Drops it.)* Wow.

SAM. *(Off, can't quite hear her.)* What is it, hon? What are you saying?

SCOOTER. Either I've got to have my eyes rechecked—or your penmanship's amazing! *(Rises, puts her robe on and becomes aware of her waist as she ties the sash.)* Now what? *(Feels waist—the front, sides and front again.)* Sam! Have I been eating right? I think I've lost some weight! *(As her hands move up towards her full bosom, looks down and reacts.)* Or did I *gain* some?

SAM. *(Off, really can't hear her.)* What? I've got the water running.

SCOOTER. *(As strange as all this seems to her, manages to shake it off and raps on bathroom door on passing.)* Will you be in there long, dear? I've got to wash my hair. *(Opens trunks, removes two blouses, a pair of blue jeans and a hatchet—which she stares at with no idea what it's doing there—before she calls out:)* Do you remember where I packed— *(Remembers.)* Never mind!

(She drops everything back in trunk, closes it, goes to closet and stoops to open a suitcase, thereby disappearing from view as SAM reenters, wearing a dress shirt and slacks.)

SAM. All yours, hon! I'll finish up out here. Oh!

(On noticing he doesn't have a tie, he returns to bathroom.)

SCOOTER. *(Pops up, shampoo and towel in her hands.)* It's all right! I'll use the kitchen!

(As she exits into kitchen, he reenters putting the tie around his neck.)

SAM. I don't really need the bathroom without a mirror ....

SCOOTER. *(Off.)* Who *does?*

SAM. But didn't you say yesterday you were just dying to take a shower? Come on! As long as you've thrown me out—!

SCOOTER. *(Off, growls good-humoredly.)* Oh ... all right!

(Though the tie is still untied, SAM notices the open bed and bends low over it to convert it back into a sofa; SCOOTER reenters just as he bends.)

SCOOTER. Honey, I've been having some of the strangest feelings...!

SAM. *(Pleased.)* You too, huh?

SCOOTER. Do you suppose it could be last night?

SAM. *(The true romantic.)* Last night in retrospective, tonight in anticipation.

SCOOTER. Well ... maybe.

(She continues into bathroom and SAM, the conversion complete, catches the quickest glimpse—more an impression than anything else—of her disappearing form.)

SAM. *(Having reacted, calls uncertainly:)* Amy....

SCOOTER. *(Off.)* Yes, hon?

SAM. When you make your next eye appointment ... will you make one for me too?

SCOOTER. *(Off.)* The shower's running! Now *I* can't hear *you!* While you're waiting, why don't you run out for a paper?

SAM. I'd really like to ... but it just isn't the same if they're not carrying my stuff. *(Notices TV and brightens with a better idea.)* Maybe *All My Children*'s on.

(He clicks TV on and now would tie the tie, but we barely hear a sound bite before there is banging and rattling at porch door.)

IRMA. *(Off.)* Mr. Galway! Yoo hoo!

SAM. *(Turns sound down to a faint murmur, goes to door and opens it.)* Yes, madam?

(IRMA PRY stands in doorway. A woman of uncertain age who is too familiar to be friendly, she wears heavy makeup, a red wig, slacks and a tight sweater.)

IRMA. Hey, call me Irma, kid. *(Shows him a small, brightly colored umbrella.)* Did you and your little Amy leave this on the porch last night?

SAM. Yeah, I guess—Ugh!

(Reacts as she carelessly thrusts it at him, forcing him to grab it lest he be impaled.)

IRMA. Makes the neighborhood look bad, y'know? Makes the Sunshine State look bad! Hey, I'm from across the court. Barney Pry's my husband.

SAM. *(Does not recognize the name.)* Barney Pry?

IRMA. *(Pulls him halfway out.)* That sly old geezer sitting on the porch there—oh, he's looking at you! Wave at him! *(With her manipulating his arm, SAM awkwardly waves umbrella.)* Oh, he appreciates that *so much!*

SAM. *(Not so sure.)* I notice he didn't wave back.

IRMA. He appreciates it where it counts—in his gut. Hey, I ain't seen any of the new wing yet. Mind if I come in?

SAM. *(Doubtful.)* Well ....

IRMA. *(Entering regardless.)* Oh, this is *nice,* Sam! You don't mind if I call you Sam, do you? It's just like *our* place except you've got a lousy color scheme.

SAM. *(Any excuse to get her out.)* We're not exactly dressed here....

IRMA. Sam, you're dressed just great! Except for that tacky tie, of course— *(In a trice she has it off him.)* But nobody wears ties here. And if little Amy isn't dressed—hey, I was a shower room attendant almost thirty years before I got lucky and married Barney. Guess how old I am!

SAM. Well ....

IRMA. Go ahead! You'll never get it.

SAM. Eighty?

IRMA. *(Incensed.)* Eighty?! *(But quickly opts for a different attitude.)* I see you're teasing me. I am forty-six.

SAM. *(Incredulous.)* Forty-six?

IRMA. It's hard to believe, sure—most take me for forty. And when I'm with my Barney—he's pushing triple figures, that's how we made the age cut—they think I'm even younger! Hey, when I drove us down from Jersey City—thirteen hours flat, including radar busts—Jeff, that cute little Jeff you met last night?—he tells me, "One of you *must* be over 55." Thought I was only *thirty,* he tells me later!—Course, it was pitch dark out and he ain't seen my Barney yet, who's laying under the furniture in the back of the SUV. But Barney's lots more active now we're all moved in. Rain or shine he's out on our porch most every day, taking in everything—*everything*—you betcha. Saw *you* stumble up your stairs last night— *(Again looking about, perhaps for her real interest.)* but he couldn't quite see, uh, your pretty bride. *(She has started for bathroom but he verbalizes an "Uhhh"—while managing to block her way; and she, affecting boredom, pretends not to notice.)* Me? I spend most of *my* time down at the swimming pool where I have to fight off the, uh, more mobile of the gentlemen. *(Touches wig:)* Would you believe?, they call me "Copperhead"—like they're afraid I might slither up and bite them! *(Coquettishly confides:)* Which one day I just might! *(Feigning a yawn.)* But of course I'm home with Barney every night. *(Beat.)* So what the hell. *(Having checked inside the top of her sweater and found an empty pack of Camels, crushes it.)* Sport, you got a cigarette? It don't have to be non-filtered.

SAM. *(Who has been squirming at her non-stop chatter.)* I smoke a pipe sometimes, but—

SCOOTER. *(Off.)* Sam?

SAM. Great Scott! I forgot to get my wife her paper! *(Calling off.)* Back in just a minute, hon! *(Hands IRMA the umbrella and rushes out.)*

IRMA. *(Calling after him.)* They got 'em front of Toys 'R Us— and pick me up a deck of Camels—!

SCOOTER. *(Off.)* Sam, I have soap in my eyes! I need another washcloth! Another towel too!

IRMA. *(Searching the place.)* Don't you worry, you sweet old thing, towels are my specialty. Ah! *(Exchanges the tie and umbrella for a washcloth and towel in the closet and marches to the bathroom door.)* Hey, Amy, I was just telling your cute husband— *(Pushes door open and, without looking, hands towel and washcloth in.)* I was a shower room attendant almost thirty years, taking care of all the gals—and some fellas too! Course, as I got older, no one paid me much attention, but—boy, how *that* has changed! Now I'm the youngest thing around! *(Impatient.)* Hey, you coming out or not? Me, my husband Barney—everybody—we're just dying to meet you! So come out and say hello!

(Consummately curious and not sure what to expect, SCOOTER enters, looking fantastic, her hair wrapped in one towel, her torso in another, using the washcloth—now dampened—to take the last vestige of soap out of an eye.)

SCOOTER. *(As she lowers washcloth.)* Hello?

IRMA. *(Who has been staring and staring.)* Who the hell are *you?*

SCOOTER. *(At a loss.)* Why, I'm Amy Galway, Sam's wife.

IRMA. *(Disgusted with her.)* You've got your nerve, sister!

(IRMA exits, slamming door.)

SCOOTER. *(Entirely lost.)* Sam? Where did you *go?* What is *happening* here? *(Dabs her eye with washcloth one last time and takes a good look at her limbs.)* What happened to my arms? What happened to my *legs?* *(Finds a tiny compact in a purse, opens it and holds it close to stare into its mirror.)* Oh my, I must have slept better than I thought! My eyes don't look at *all* puffy— *(Tilting mirror.)* Oh, but my lips do. *(Frightened:)* Or are they *full* again?! *(Casts about, hyperventilating.)* Oh—! Oh—! If I only had a bigger mirror— *(Notices the murmuring TV.)* Wait! *(Goes to it and clicks it off to stare at her reflected image on the screen.)* Oh no. *(A step back to stare some more.)* Oh no. *(Another step.)* Oh no ... *no!*

SAM. *(Off, rattles door.)* Amy, I'm back!

SCOOTER. *(Screams.)* Stay away from here!

SAM. It's all right, that woman's gone. *(Rattles again.)* Let me in, will you? I don't have my key!

SCOOTER. Oh dear. Oh dear. Oh dear oh dear oh dear.

(Frantic lest he see her like this, wraps herself in his robe and covers her face with the hair towel.)

SAM. *(Off, continues rattling; teasing:)* The neighbors will think the newlyweds are having their first fight!

SCOOTER. *(Throws door open, much put out.)* I got here as fast as I could! What do you want?

SAM. *(Enters with a newspaper, surprised at her display of temper.)* Shh, dearest. That's Barney Pry across the way. Wave at him, he likes that. *(He waves and she reluctantly does too.)* But let him see your pretty face—!

(He reaches for the towel but she jumps away.)

SCOOTER. Don't you touch me!

SAM. Oh oh. *(Closes door slowly.)* Why do I feel—I'm feeling like a married man?

SCOOTER. That's right! *Laugh* at me!

SAM. *(Goes to her.)* No one's laughing at you, Amy. You just threw me a little, that's all. *(Drops paper on sofa and starts to put his arms around her; she sniffles and allows him; reassuringly:)* That's better! Clearly, I've done something awful wrong.... Oh, I know! I went out when you were calling me! But that woman—Irma Pry?—I thought she'd never *leave!* She just kept going on and on ... *(Is patting her back as he speaks but now, curiosity compelling him, lets his hand stray a little lower.)* and on ... *(A little lower.)* and on ... and— *(Beat; knowing absolutely now, he thrusts her away, demanding:)* Young woman, who are you? What do you want?

SCOOTER. *(All in tears, that word again:)* Geemanetly!
SAM. *(Astonished.) Amy?*

(He removes the towel to see her face.)

SCOOTER. *(Sobbing away.)* Ooooooh! Ooooooh! Ooooooh!
SAM. *(Stunned.)* But it *can't* be you!
SCOOTER. *(Miserable.)* Don't you think I *know* that?
SAM. *(A cry from his soul.)* Geemanetly!

(As they cling to each other, SAM beginning to sob too, there is a blackout ending the scene.)

Scene 3

(LIGHTS RISE on that evening. Various contents of the suitcases and trunk are spread about, including books and tools. Some suitcases are open but the trunk is closed and on it rests, among other things, the hatchet. L. end table holds what seems to be a pitcher full of water; r. end table holds the newspaper and compact. SAM, whose shirt is partially unbuttoned but is otherwise

dressed as we last saw him, is apparently drinking all the water he can hold. He stands d.r. just finishing a glass as SCOOTER, terribly attractive in a checkered blouse and jeans, examines a scrapbook on the sofa. On finishing it, he shakes his head and, eyes bulging but determined, moves to l. end table, picks the pitcher up and begins to pour another glass before— too desperate for half-measures—he chugalugs what he has poured, takes pitcher d.c. and seems to drain it too. At last, a hand on his stomach and eyes bulging more than ever, he sets pitcher on r. end table, picks up compact and uses its mirror to check his face—and gut—before he GROANS and sits down heavily next to SCOOTER on the sofa.)

SCOOTER. *(Who was oblivious to most the above.)* Oh, Sam! Look! Here I am at sixteen. Do you see the resemblance? Do you see it is *me? (His attention caught, he looks at photo and nods halfheartedly.)* That's my mother, my uncle Bill, and Dad. *(Another photo.)* And that's our new car, a Studebaker! See how the back—or is it the front?—looks exactly like the front—or back? *(Turns a page.)* And here I am at eighteen! That's Walford in his uniform. He was a pitcher and a catcher.

SAM. *(Surprised at this last.)* What?

SCOOTER. Oh, I used to go to *all* his games—even before I met him! *(Illustrates the following as she speaks: first the pitching, then the acceptance of the ball as it is obviously returned by a catcher.)* He'd pitch, then he'd catch ... then he'd pitch, then he'd catch ... someone would hit a homer ... *("Watches it" sail over her head.)* then he'd pitch, then he'd catch....

SAM. *(Nods sharply.)* Got it.

SCOOTER. *(Another page.)* I'm nineteen here. See? Take a look at me—in the photo and beside you! Same girl. Same girl, Sam! Is there any doubt?

SAM. *(After studying photo, takes a longer look at her, with special interest:)* So you figure you're nineteen *now?*

SCOOTER. That's what I prayed for—to return to the year when I was so desperately in love. So—yes!—I *have* to be nineteen.

SAM. Thank God. I thought you were seventeen.

(He rises, shakes his head to clear it and exits into bathroom.)

SCOOTER. *(Calls.)* Sam!

SAM. *(Off.)* Just a minute, hon—!

SCOOTER. *(Closes scrapbook, frets.)* You poor dear! *(As he returns.)* You're taking this awfully hard!

SAM. Me? What about *you?* You cried through two towels and a pillow case.

SCOOTER. Well, I was sad!

SAM. Of course! The difference in our ages—! *(She smiles up at him:)* But why aren't you sad *now?*

SCOOTER. *(As she thinks about it.)* Oh. Well. For one thing ... we sure were a big hit at the brunch.

SAM. *(Accuses her.)* *You* were the big hit, Amy! All those aging dandies hanging on your every word, offering you rides on their paddleboats and golf carts...!

SCOOTER. The women were nice too! Even that Mrs. Pry—!

SAM. *Watch* that Irma Pry! *(Confides a terrible secret.)* She's a copperhead.

SCOOTER. But she was so considerate once I told her I'd just been teasing when I said I was your wife—and was really your visiting niece, Eileen!

SAM. The "visiting" was what caught her ear. That means you'll be leaving.

SCOOTER. Well, I *will*, won't I? This can't go on forever.

SAM. Isn't that what they said about the Rolling Stones?

SCOOTER. *(Ignores this.)* Barney—Irma's husband?—I really kind of liked. She said it was the first time she could get him off the porch in weeks.

SAM. Get him *off* it? She couldn't keep him *on* it once he saw *you* come prancing down our stairs. Do you have any idea—any real idea—of what you look like now?

SCOOTER. *(Although fearing the answer:)* Why don't you *tell* me?

SAM. Amy, you're the final fantasy of every old man's dreams. You're life, you're radiance, you're youth. Just seeing you brings new strength to aging arms, fresh air to gasping lungs and rich red blood to old, discouraged hearts. You are life—and worse than life. You are life's reminder: how it was and—for most of us—will never be again. *(Moved by his words, she stands quite close to him.)* And ... you're one thing more.

SCOOTER. *(Fears this answer too.)* What's that, Sam?

SAM. You're the biggest story of the century and I can't call it in!

(He moves away in sheer frustration.)

SCOOTER. *(Follows.)* But why *can't* you?—if that's what you really want to do!

SAM. Who would believe it?! And how could I explain—if that Fountain of Youth did spring up, you're the only one got splashed?

SCOOTER. But it makes so much sense! The terrible rain, a brand new well, new plumbing in our bathroom! The water got in there somehow—and, of the two of us, I was the one who had a glass.

SAM. *(Groans.)* But I've had a *thousand* glasses since! *(Reminded.)* Excuse me. *(Re-exits into bathroom, closing door.)*

SCOOTER. *(Follows to the door.)* Don't run away in the middle of our—! Is this our *real* first fight, Sam?

SAM. *(Off.)* Don't be silly, Amy.

SCOOTER. *(Hurt.)* Now I'm being *silly?* You didn't seem to think so last night! You *brought* me that water, remember? You *wanted* it to work! You wanted your girl of nineteen again—and you *know* you did!

SAM. *(Appears in doorway and says with difficulty:)* If I did, for just a moment there ... well, that moment's gone. I did not expect to wake up with a child bride.

SCOOTER. *(Challenges him.)* Didn't you? Or isn't that what you *really* wanted? Your young and beautiful Miss Quimby again! *(He simply looks at her; then after a moment.)* All right, you don't have to get nasty about it. *(Bumps into trunk and, kicking it, demands:)* Can't we do something about this stupid trunk?! *(Sits and after a moment adds:)* I wonder how long it lasts.

SAM. *(In his own thoughts.)* Hmm?

SCOOTER. This miracle—scientific breakthrough—whatever the heck it is. Is it like the chicken pox, you get it and it goes away? Do you snap back to what you were—age from where you are? Or do you stay *nineteen*? *(On her feet again.)* Don't get me wrong, it's not that bad an age. Here the sun's gone down and for the first time in years my every bone's not screaming for a Tylenol and mattress. But there are things I just as soon would skip if I have to take the long way back. *(Touching her teeth.)* Four years in the dentist's chair ... seven years of hot flashes ... and watching any movie starring Cheech and Chong.

SAM. *(Feeling bad for her.)* Amy, I am sorry.

SCOOTER. Sure you are.

SAM. I am! Here I've been thinking about my own fears and ignoring yours.

SCOOTER. *(Surprised at his admission.)* But I don't understand.... What fears could *you* have?

SAM. *(Equivocates.)* Fear—well—it has so much to do with the unknown—that I don't know if I know enough to tell you.

SCOOTER. It isn't that you're *scared* to tell me—! *(With insight.)* Are you *that* scared, Sam?

SAM. *(Would dismiss this.)* There you go, being silly again. I am fine, Amy. Really.

SCOOTER. *(Decides to accept this.)* All right—good! For a moment there I thought you might be worried about my date with Jeff.

SAM. *(Stunned.) What date with Jeff?*

SCOOTER. I told you!

SAM. You did *not!*

SCOOTER. *(Points at TV.)* I said it loud and clear when you were watching *As the World Turns.*

SAM. *(Guilty.) Oh.*

SCOOTER. See, when Irma corralled me at the brunch this morning, she asked an *awful* lot of questions. Like what did I do in Milwaukee? What was I doing *here?* Where would I be sleeping? And, uh, when would Amy—Aunt Amy, I should say—be up and about again?

SAM. *(With concern.)* What did you tell her?

SCOOTER. Why, the truth, of course.

SAM. *(Astonished.)* The *truth?*

SCOOTER. Nearly as I could. I said I was a student, studying nutrition at Marquette—because I actually did that, see? I said I'd come here as a surprise, that you and Aunt Amy weren't expecting me—because we certainly were not! And I said we didn't know *when* she would be able to meet her, but we hoped it would be soon—and I meant it with all my heart!

SAM. *(Zeroes in on the point of her avoidance.)* Where did you say you'd sleep?

SCOOTER. Oh that. Well … I said … *(So quietly we almost do not hear her.)* I'd sleep in town.

SAM. *(No trouble hearing him.) Where?*

SCOOTER. In town! What *could* I say? There isn't room for the three of us in here!

SAM. You may have a point but— *(Leery.) where* in town exactly?

SCOOTER. *(In an apologetic rush.)* That's just what Irma said and, not knowing the hotels, I said I wasn't sure yet, so she said not only would Jeff's folks put me for almost nothing but he'd run me back and forth besides and I said, "Gee, that'd be nice, but—" but I couldn't even get the "but" out before she was calling him over to arrange a ride and suddenly he's saying, "Great, my folks are throwing me a party and you can be my special guest." Anyhow— *(Beat.)* that's how I got the date.

SAM. *(Whose head is in his hands by now, slowly raises it.)* You are *not* going out with him.

SCOOTER. *(Intimidated.)* Oh, I'm not!... Why not?

SAM. *(Explodes.)* Because you *can't,* that's why! This is our honeymoon!

SCOOTER. But it isn't! I mean, it *is,* but it's really yours and old Aunt Amy's. And how could I say I'd be sleeping *here* when we only have one bed?

SAM. So I'll get a cot!

SCOOTER. Get *two* cots! Get a hundred! As long as there's just you and me inside this little love nest— *(Draws herself up to the height of her indignation.)* people will *talk!*

SAM. *(Eyes so narrowed he is almost Machiavellian.)* But people think there are *three* of us—you, me and old Aunt Amy. So they might think *you* slept on the cot or *I* slept on the cot, but they won't think *she* slept on the cot. Her aching bones can't *stand* it!

SCOOTER. Oh. Yeah. I guess.... *(Wistful.)* It sure sounded like a nice party though. It turns out Jeff collects sixteen-millimeter films: Buster Keaton, Laurel and Hardy—all of my old favorites. *(Checks to see if he has relented; one look tells her he has not.)* But, like I said, I won't be going. *(Sighs.)* I'll stay home and watch you watch TV.

SAM. *(Goes to her.)* Honey, I hate to disappoint you, but you've got to realize—though you certainly have the mind of my dear, sweet Amy, you've the body, hormones and probably emotions of a nineteen-year-old girl. Watching movies in the dark beside some good-looking young man—

SCOOTER. *(Shocked.)* You don't think I'd be anything less than one hundred percent faithful to you!?

SAM. No! Of course not! Never in a million years! *(Beat.)* But why take the chance?

SCOOTER. ... You could be right.

SAM. Trust me.

SCOOTER. *(Pouts.)* Trust *you!* Huh.

(A knock at the door.)

SAM. *(As he starts for it.)* If that's Jeff—

SCOOTER. *I'll* tell him—please! *(Her plea is such that he backs off and sits on sofa; a quick reminder:)* You know what to call me while he's here.

SAM. Eileen. Right.

SCOOTER. *(Beat.)* That'll do. *(With SAM wondering about this last, she opens door.)* Hello, Jeff!

(JEFF stands in doorway, still dressed as he was last night, but now moonstruck and woebegone, a valentine of smiles and lost young love.)

JEFF. Hi, Scooter.

SAM. *(First he's heard this.)* Scooter?

(She gives SAM a look and he pretends to read the paper.)

JEFF. Like, I won't be ready to leave for a few minutes, but I wanted to stop by and—

SCOOTER. Come in, won't you?

JEFF. Sure. *(Enters and we see he carries a box of candy.)* See, I hoped to— *(Noticing SAM.)* Oh, hi, Mr. Galway. How are *you* this evening?

SAM. *(Deep in paper, a noncommittal grunt:)* Mmm.

JEFF. The, uh—person I really came to see— *(Looks around.)* Where is *Mrs.* Galway? *(Starts toward open bathroom door.)*

SCOOTER. Jeff! Don't! *(As he stops, she hurries past him to the door.)* Aunt Amy, we have company! You really ought to keep this closed. *(On closing door, to JEFF.)* She forgets sometimes.

SAM. *(Still deep in paper.)* The poor old thing.

JEFF. *(Concern.)* Is it true she was sick?

SCOOTER. Not too badly—

SAM. *(Simultaneously as he looks up from paper.)* Very. *(With JEFF staring questions at them.)* Guess it all depends what "was" was.

SCOOTER. Sam!

(He returns to paper.)

JEFF. *(Though confused by these strange answers.)* Anyhow—I brought these for her.

SAM. *(Looking up again.)* Amy hates sweets, Jeff—hasn't eaten them in years.

JEFF. Ohh. Then, uh…?

(Needing to do something with the candy, tentatively extends it to SCOOTER.)

SAM. I told you, she—

SCOOTER. *(Cuts in lest he say too much.)* Thank you, Jeff! I *love* sweets—and I always have!

SAM. *(Mutters darkly.)* Wait till you see what they do your teeth.

JEFF. *(For her ears alone.)* Mr Galway—he isn't feeling too well either?

SCOOTER. *(For JEFF's ears alone.)* He's upset, naturally, because of what his wife is going through.

JEFF. What's she going through?

SCOOTER. We're not exactly sure … but we hope it is just temporary.

JEFF. Me too, Scooter. *(Remembers.)* Oh! I'm supposed to let her know: Everyone so missed seeing her at the brunch today, if she's up and about, they'll throw another one for her tomorrow!

SCOOTER. *(Curious.)* How about *you*, Jeff? Did *you* miss seeing her?

JEFF. Oh yeah—a lot. But you more or less made up for it.

SAM. *(Who looked up during this last.)* Will you two talk louder or softer?! I'm getting every other word and it's driving me crazy.

SCOOTER. Sorry, Sam! *(To JEFF.)* Listen, about tonight—I cannot stay in town.

JEFF. *(Frowns.)* You can't?

SAM. She can't!

SCOOTER. *(Apologetically to JEFF.)* I really can't.

JEFF. *No problemo,* Scooter. I'll just you bring you back here when the party's over.

(JEFF starts toward door but SCOOTER takes his upper arms in what, to an intruder, might appear to be the beginning or the end of an embrace.)

SCOOTER. But you don't understand! See—

(IRMA intrudes with a soup tureen, JEFF having left the door open.)

IRMA. Ha! I caught you— *(But now sees SAM and hardly missing a beat, adds:)* Home, I mean! So, where's the sick old lady?

JEFF. *(Helpful.)* Mrs. Galway's in the bathroom, ma'am.

IRMA. *(Finds this curious.)* That's where she— *(Realizes; to SCOOTER.)* no, *you*—were the last time I came by. *(Already at bathroom door.)* Amy, darling! I have soup for you!

SAM. No! Wait!

(But he speaks too late; she has exited into bathroom and the door has closed.)

JEFF. *(Unaware of the frantic looks exchanged by SAM and SCOOTER, would resume the conversation.)* All right, what don't I understand?

SCOOTER. Nothing! Nothing at all! *(Would push him out the door.)* Go!

JEFF. But—you'll be coming *down* soon? Or do you want me to come back *up?*

SCOOTER. Whatever! Whatever! Yes!

(JEFF exits and she closes the door.)

SAM. *(Who has found his feet.)* You're not going *out* with him!?

SCOOTER. I had to tell him *something!* How else are we going to—

(SCOOTER sees IRMA who, though impeded by the tureen she is holding with both hands, manages to reopen bathroom door and is backing into scene; SCOOTER, thinking wildly, rushes to the phone, getting the receiver to her ear just as IRMA turns to face them.)

SCOOTER. *(On the phone.)* That's terrible! She *is?*

IRMA. There isn't anybody in the—

SCOOTER. She *did?* Just *now?*

IRMA. *(At once caught up in the drama.)* What is it? What's happening?

SCOOTER. Oh my goodness! *(Covers mouthpiece.)* Poor Aunt Amy! She fell down again!

IRMA. *(Terribly confused.)* Where? She isn't in the tub....

SCOOTER. In the bathroom—in the hospital!

IRMA. *(Putting it together.)* She's in the *hospital* bathroom! Oh!

SCOOTER. *(To SAM, distressed.)* They keep trying to pick her *up* but she keeps falling *down!*

IRMA. Is she slippery?

SCOOTER. *(Shushing her.)* Wait a minute. Yes, doctor? She *did? (Beat.)* She *isn't? (Beat.)* Oh, that's wonderful!

(SCOOTER hangs up.)

IRMA. *(Repeating SCOOTER's words.) What* did she? What *isn't* she?

SAM. I'd like to know myself.

SCOOTER. She, uh ... got up under her own power.

IRMA. That's "She did."

SCOOTER. And she *isn't* ... sick any more.

SAM. What a relief!

(He sits and covers his face with a hand.)

IRMA. *(Consumed with curiosity.)* How exactly was she sick?

SCOOTER. Well ... she was lying on the floor ... and she couldn't get back up....

IRMA. In the bathroom? In the hospital? That's what she was there for—because she was lying on the floor? But why was she there if she wasn't sick before she *got* there?

SCOOTER. *(Weakly.)* She does lots of volunteer work.

IRMA. On her *honeymoon?*

SCOOTER. My Aunt Amy is an extremely selfless woman.

IRMA. *(Trying to recall.)* But didn't you say ... she was sick this *morning?*

SCOOTER. No, I said she wasn't "up and about." See, what happened this morning—

SAM. *(Helpful.)* That's when she fell on the floor.

IRMA. *(Lost.)* I don't understand this! She fell on the floor, in the hospital, this morning—and they're just picking her up *now?*

SCOOTER. *(A grasp at any straw.)* But nobody knew she was *on* the floor. That's why it took so long!

IRMA. I thought you said *you* knew.

SCOOTER. We were the only ones—and she didn't want us blabbing it all over town!

IRMA. *(Progressively more suspicious.)* Wait a minute! Wait a minute!... What hospital is she at?

SCOOTER. Hospital? Oh, I'm terrible with names!... Sam?

SAM. *(Having retreated behind the paper.)* I'm afraid it slipped my mind.

IRMA. *(Nobody's fool.)* Something funny's going on here. *(Sets tureen on trunk.)* You're on a honeymoon, your wife is volunteering at a hospital, you don't know which one, but you're talking to her on the phone while she's laying on a bathroom floor which nobody knows she's on except you—and you. And you don't tell the doctors and the nurses? You don't go and *get* her? *(Takes SAM's paper.)* Hey you—I'm *talking* to you!

SAM. Yes, I see you are—and my niece has a perfectly rational explanation.

IRMA. She'd better!

SCOOTER. We, uh, didn't tell the doctors and the nurses because we didn't know which hospital she's at. We didn't know which hospital—because *she* called *us—!*

SAM. *(Impressed.)* So far so good.

SCOOTER. Naturally, we *asked* her where she was but, as I said, she's extremely selfless and wouldn't say unless we promised not to make a fuss. Besides—she wasn't hurt.

IRMA. She wasn't?

SAM. *(Indignant.)* Do you think we'd leave her on the floor if she was *hurt?!*

SCOOTER. All she needed was a rest! And she knew that *someone* would come along *eventually.* Praise the Lord, that's finally what happened!

SAM. *(Quietly.)* Hallelujah.

IRMA. *(More suspicious than ever, returns to trunk for the tureen, notices hatchet, picks it up and "weighs" it—haft in one hand, blade in the other—perhaps wondering how it might fit into the puzzle as she asks:)* When does she get out?

SCOOTER. Of the hospital? Oh, I don't know. Tonight—tomorrow—soon.

IRMA. *(Standing over SAM with hatchet.)* Well, it *better* be soon. Do you get my drift, Sam?

SAM. Madam, will you kindly put that hatchet down?

IRMA. Yeah, *real* soon—and I ain't kidding. *(Returns hatchet to the trunk.)* We got laws in this here state against cohabitation—among some other things. And if I thought for a minute you and your so-called niece—

(As IRMA picks tureen up, there is a knock on the door.)

JEFF. *(Off.)* Eilee-een! *(SCOOTER freezes, as does SAM; more knocking.)* Scooter! Are you ready?

IRMA. *(Studies her.)* I believe it's time for your date, my dear. You *do* have a date with Jeff, don't you?

SCOOTER. Huh! Well! Hmm!

(A frantic look at SAM.)

JEFF. *(Off, more knocking.)* Scooter!

SAM. Oh, blast it all! *(Having risen, pushes door open to admit JEFF, who has changed from his whites into casual clothes and looks very nice indeed.)* Scooter's ready, fella.

SCOOTER. *(Implores SAM.)* But—are you sure?

JEFF. Come on, Scoot, everybody will be waiting!

SCOOTER. *(Touches SAM's arm.)* I'll be back—just as early as I can!

JEFF. Good night, Mr. Galway!

SCOOTER. Good night, Sam!

(Though upset and perhaps frightened, SCOOTER exits with JEFF.)

IRMA. *(None too pleasantly.)* Good *night*, Sam.

(IRMA follows the two out.)

SAM. *(At door, more lost than ever, tentatively waves at each.)* Good night, Jeff ... Scooter ... Irma ... *(Raising a hand to wave at someone in the distance:)* Barney! *(Closes door.)* And good night, St. Dymphna—wherever you are.

(SAM's head is in his hands again as lights fall on Act I.)

ACT II

Scene 1

(It is a few hours later. Lights rise to the dimness of the ambient light from outside—and we hear someone at porch door.)

JEFF. *(Off.)* Scoot....
SCOOTER. *(Off.)* Shhh!

(She gets door open and they enter.)

JEFF. I still don't see—
SCOOTER. Quiet, Jeff!

(She closes door.)

JEFF. *(Somewhat quieter.)* I still don't see why we had to wait in my car until the Prys turned off their lights!

SCOOTER. Not so loud—please! We don't want to wake up— *(Clicks l. lamp on—lights rise enough to let us see the bed is open but SAM is nowhere in sight.)* Sam??? *(As she looks about, we also see that the earlier mess has been straightened up, the suitcases are put away and the trunk is gone.)* Where could he ...? *(Goes to kitchen doorway.)* Sam? *(Turns r. lamp on, lights rising to full, and crosses to the open bathroom door.)* Honey? *(Next checks closet.)* His clothes are here, thank God.

JEFF. You didn't think they *would* be?

43

SCOOTER. Yes, but I thought *he'd* be here too! Where can anyone go around Fountain Springs at two o'clock in the morning?

JEFF. Gee, I don't— *(Remembers.)* Dog night!

SCOOTER. I beg your pardon?

JEFF. Tonight's dog night—the track! A whole busload was headed there. He probably went with.

SCOOTER. *(Doubtful.)* He never told me he liked dog races.

JEFF. Must've been *her* idea.

SCOOTER. Whose?

JEFF. Mrs. Galway, who'dja think? You don't see *her* here, do you?

SCOOTER. *(Recovering.)* Oh, yes—no, I don't.

JEFF. Sometimes, you know, the women like the dogs even more than men.

SCOOTER. *(A gentle correction.)* More than the men *do.*

JEFF. Yeah, that too. *(Beat.)* Anyway, you're safely home.

(He starts for door.)

SCOOTER. Jeff! *(A little nervous.)* If you don't mind too much—could you stay here just till Sam gets back?

JEFF. *(Nervous for a different reason.)* Well ....

SCOOTER. I'll make you some coffee—I make a good cup of coffee, Jeff.

JEFF. I'll bet you do. You're a whizbang in the kitchen, according to my Mom. She never knew anyone your age, she said, who could whip up chicken cacciatore for thirty-seven people.

SCOOTER. I'm used to lots of people, I guess—but I'm also used to just one. Let me make that coffee!

(She exits into kitchen and turns its light on.)

JEFF. She also said I ought to snap you up—that she was amazed, after the movies, how badly you beat the rest of us at trivia—

how you came right out with John Wayne's real name, Cary Grant's real name, Jimmy Stewart's real name— *(Beat.)* What was it?

SCOOTER. *(Off.)* Jimmy Stewart.

JEFF. Right! And how you knew Baby Snooks' little brother's name was Robespierre—?!

(He throws his hands up in amazement.)

SCOOTER. *(Appears in kitchen doorway.)* I had a classical education.

JEFF. *(Has to know.)* And tonight? Did you have a decent time?

SCOOTER. Oh Jeff! It was wonderful! Being around all those young people! I'd forgotten how much fun it can be!

JEFF. Don't get around young people much, huh?

SCOOTER. Not lately. No.

JEFF. *(Admits.)* I had a pretty good time myself. But it wasn't the young people—not all of them, Scooter— *(Noticing how close she is, backs a little.)* Think that coffee's about ready?

SCOOTER. *(Curious.)* What is it? Are you uncomfortable around me?

JEFF. Oh, for gosh sakes, no! Why would you say— *(As he further backs up, he trips on open bed, falls on it, scrambles to his feet and almost knocks lamp over, having to steady it with both hands before he lamely adds:)* a thing like that?

SCOOTER. The thought did cross my mind, that's all. *(Smiles.)* I'll get the coffee.

(She disappears back into kitchen.)

JEFF. Scooter?... Eileen?... *(She returns with two mugs.)* It isn't that I'm uncomfortable around *you.* It's like young people in general I'm uncomfortable around. That's why my folks threw me the party. They hoped I'd get to know some.

SCOOTER. I don't understand.

JEFF. See, I work in this place all the time, more hours than I have to. Before that, I was away at school. You may not have noticed but almost everybody there tonight were children of my parents' friends. I just don't know a lot of kids my age. And most of the ones I do—well, I just don't care for.

SCOOTER. Are you saying you don't care for *me?*

JEFF. You? Oh no. You're different.

SCOOTER. *(Wonders about this.)* How?

JEFF. Well, when we played music trivia, for instance, you beat us all at naming the swing era bands and singers, but then, when we moved into early rock 'n' roll—it's like you never *heard* of Led Zeppelin and KISS. *(She is looking at him blankly.)* I'll bet you don't even know who the Doors were!

SCOOTER. The who?

JEFF. No, that's another group.

SCOOTER. *(Did not know this either.)* Ohh.

JEFF. *(Tries to explain.)* But it's all right, I *like* older tastes—older things—especially older people. I mean, they've got so much more going for them than young people do! They're relaxed about so many things that drive young people crazy! Take making out, for instance. Old people, they couldn't care less about it—most of them—at least half the time. Fame? They'd trade their fifteen minutes worth for a fifteen-minute nap. Ambition? Travel? If they're not already there—they just don't want to go! Study old people when you get the chance. Zits on their noses mean nothing in the world to them. Are they too small, too tall, too thin, too fat? They don't care any more about *that* than the way they look in jeans. As for money—yeah, they like it all right. But what they really want to do with it is buy things for their grandkids. Young people aren't that way. No, they're not at all.

SCOOTER. *(Who has been listening, fascinated.)* All old people aren't that way either.

JEFF. All right, so sometimes age *is* wasted on the old. But so many try to make each day count, now that their days are numbered.

And they'll tell you, if you ask them, that the only worthwhile goals in life are to get as far away from time clocks and near to heaven as you can! They *are* near to heaven, Scooter. I'm very comfortable around them.

SCOOTER. *(Appreciating him.)* I'm beginning to see why.

JEFF. Scooter—Eileen—did it ever occur to you— *(Dares to take her hand.)* you might consider growing *old* with me at Fountain Springs?

SCOOTER. *(Astonished.)* Jeff! *(As it sinks in:)* You just made my day, my year, my—oh my oh my!

JEFF. Well, would—?

SCOOTER. Under different circumstances—assuming we had the time to really get to know each other—well, I'd certainly consider it.

JEFF. But we've lots of time—our entire lives ahead! If you could just stick around here for a while—

SCOOTER. That's the point, I can't. I may have to leave this place very, very suddenly. And when I do—I'll never, never be able to come back. That's just the way it is. I'm sorry.

JEFF. *(So glum he can't help pouting.)* You seem to care about my caring for *you*—but *you* don't care for *me!*

SCOOTER. *(Tenderly.)* Oh, Jeff! I know a lot of girls have said this to a lot of fellows—but, in so many ways, I'm so much older than you are.

JEFF. *(Protests.)* But I *like* older women!

SCOOTER. Then find a *young* one and stick with her, no matter what. She'll be older—you will too—faster than you can imagine. It's one of the sweetest—and lousiest—mysteries of life.

JEFF. *(Notices red liquid on the floor, his face darkening.)* Speaking of mysteries …. Ooo, is that blood?

SCOOTER. *(Horrified.)* Blood?

JEFF. Don't touch it! *(A closer look.)* Yeah ... it's blood all right.

SCOOTER. But whose? *(Looks frantically around.)* Sam! Where *are* you???

(A knock on door; both jump and nearly scream before:)

SAM. *(Off, a hoarse whisper.)* Honey, are you in there? You shot the dead bolt.

SCOOTER. *(Relieved.)* Sam!

(SCOOTER rushes to door and opens it.)

SAM. *(Enters with hatchet and a folding cot—one of those canvas-and-stick affairs—and a super-large bandage on one finger.)* Would you believe it? I had to rent a car and drive through forty miles of swamp just to *find* this blasted thing.

(He closes door.)

SCOOTER. *(Warning him.)* We have company.

SAM. *(Not sure he likes this.)* Yeah, I see we do.

SAM & SCOOTER. *(As it occurs to them, together:)* Where's Aunt Amy?

SAM. Isn't she still in—

SCOOTER. *(All but simultaneous.)* Didn't she go out with *you?*

SAM. Come to think of it—that's right, she did! But she got tired—it was a long, hard drive—so I had to drop her off.

SCOOTER. *(Before she can stop herself.)* Where?

SAM. *(Does not appreciate her help.)* At the— *(A glance at JEFF.)* Holiday Inn?

JEFF. Sure, there's one in *town*.

SAM. *(Nods, relieved.)* I thought there might be. There's two in Kenosha.

(He starts to assemble the cot in the area where the trunk was.)

SCOOTER. *(As she notices.)* Oh! You cut your finger!

SAM. *(Working.)* Cut it? I darn near chopped it off. That's another reason I went out—six stitches and a tetanus shot. *(Perplexed, examines one of the sticks.)* Shouldn't there be a hole here?

JEFF. Let me have a look.

(JEFF stoops to help and, for all practical purposes, takes over the assembly.)

SCOOTER. What were you trying to chop, Sam?

SAM. The trunk, what did you think? There wasn't room for it *and* the cot in here. Finally had to drag the darn thing out. *(Straightens up with difficulty; aside to her, regarding JEFF.)* Did you *really* want *two* cots? Is he spending the night?

SCOOTER. No, of course not! He helped me wait, that's all.

SAM. Helped you wait?... I see.

JEFF. *(Rises, the stick that perplexed SAM in his hand.)* You're right about the hole, sir. We're going to need a drill.

SAM. Drills are in short supply here. But if a hatchet will help....

(SAM picks it up.)

JEFF. It's OK. I've got one in my car.

(JEFF exits.)

SCOOTER. *(At once embraces her husband.)* Oh Sam, thank you! Thank you so very much for letting me go out with Jeff! I learned so many things tonight—!

SAM. *(Not sure he likes this.)* Did you?

SCOOTER. I admit he taught me some—but mostly I taught myself.

SAM. It must've been some date.

SCOOTER. It was! And do you know? With all that's happened,

good and bad, today just has to be—one of my best days ever!

SAM. *(Sighs.)* The day I was held hostage in the Post Office was a better day for me.

SCOOTER. *(Suddenly aware of his attitude and condition.)* Are you all right? Can I get you a Tylenol or aspirin?

SAM. Naw, I never use that stuff unless I've got a really splitting headache—and I'm too numb for that right now.

SCOOTER. How about some coffee then?

SAM. It'd probably just un-numb me and bring the headache on.

SCOOTER. *(As she steers him toward the bed.)* At least, lie down! We'll pretend the cot's for me. After Jeff goes, I'll crawl in next to you and—

SAM. *(Stops abruptly.)* I don't think so. Not tonight.

SCOOTER. *(Startled.)* I'm sorry?

SAM. *(The truth at last.)* It just isn't any good, that's all, with you the way you are! *(Turns her to face TV.)* Look at us! I'm a doddering old man who can't even chop a box up without darn near self-assassination. And you—you're Playmate of the Month.

SCOOTER. But I *belong* to you! I belong *with* you!

SAM. I don't know where *either* of us belong … but I don't think it's anywhere around each other.

SCOOTER. *(Tears beginning.)* Sam! That's a *terrible* thing to say!

SAM. Amy, this morning I used the phrase: "Last night in retrospection, tonight in anticipation." But since then I've been anticipating tonight about the way I anticipated gall bladder surgery.

SCOOTER. *(Her heart pierced.)* Sam!

SAM. There's something so *wrong* about it!

SCOOTER. Was it wrong last night?

SAM. No, of course not, but—

SCOOTER. Honey, I've spent all day trying to undo whatever it was we did! I said every prayer I could think of, drank orange juice, coffee—water too! I've done or undone it all—except for just one thing.

SAM. *(Gets her meaning, shocked.)* Amy!

SCOOTER. Well, hasn't it occurred to you that *that* might be the missing factor—the one thing we have left to do to bring Aunt Amy back? Whatever I may look like, I'm still your wife, you know, the same sweet girl you married. And don't forget, you took me for richer or poorer, for better or for worse—

SAM. But not for *younger,* Amy! *(She starts to cry.)* Sweetheart ... dearest ... I know what you're saying ... and you know the last thing I'd ever want to do is disappoint you. But the way I feel right now—I'd disappoint you no matter what. *(Sits heavily on bed.)* Call me if there's a fire or the copperheads attack. Anything else—I'm sorry, but I'm beat.

(He swings legs around and lies down.)

SCOOTER. *(Miserable.)* Oh Sam! *(A knock on door; she pulls herself together and opens it.)* Come in, Jeff. You might as well.
HOWARD. *(Off.)* Sorry. It isn't Jeff.
SCOOTER. Oh?

(SCOOTER backs up as HOWARD enters.)

SAM. *(Struggles to sit up.)* Howard?
HOWARD. Sam, I hate to do it—but I've been asked to place you under arrest.
SAM. *(On his feet, can't believe it.)* Under arrest? What for? Whatever it may look like—there is absolutely no "cohabitation" going on here!
HOWARD. Maybe not, but— *(Takes a breath.)* the crime I've been asked to arrest you for is ... murder.
SAM. *(After a pause, to SCOOTER.)* On second thought, I'll have two aspirins, four Tylenols—and all the coffee you can make.

(SCOOTER looks at SAM, who looks at HOWARD, who keeps a care-

ful eye on both and there is a blackout.)

Scene 2

(Lights rise on same scene an instant later. All is exactly as we last saw it, the three remaining frozen in their positions until:)

SAM: *(Impatient.)* Well? Are you going to get me that coffee or not?

SCOOTER. *(Snaps to.)* Oh sure, Sam. *(Starts for kitchen.)* Back in just a—

IRMA. *(Enters with a warning.)* I wouldn't let her leave the room!

HOWARD. Mrs. Pry! I asked you to wait outside.

IRMA. It's Irma, kid, and I'd *stay* outside if you'd do your job! *(Meaning SAM:) He* should be in cuffs by now!

SAM. *(Menace in his voice as he takes a step in her direction.)* Suppose *I* ask you to wait outside?

IRMA. He's threatening me! Do you see that evil glint in his right eye? Where's that axe? Draw your gun—stop him!

HOWARD. *(Interposes himself between the two.)* Now nobody's threatening anybody ... but I will put *this* aside. *(Uses handkerchief to move hatchet from where SAM left it to beyond SAM's reach; to SCOOTER:)* The coffee will have to wait, miss. *(Indicating bed.)* Sit down, won't you? You too, Sam.

(SAM and SCOOTER sit on bed.)

IRMA. What about me? I'm the key witness!

HOWARD. All right, you sit too.

IRMA. *(Starts toward r. arm chair but stops.)* Shouldn't I get Barney? He's almost as key as I am.

HOWARD. *(In a voice that brooks no argument.) Sit,* Irma.

IRMA. Yes sir.

(IRMA meekly sits and JEFF enters with a drill.)

JEFF. *(Surprised to see them.)* Sheriff Monteith? Mrs. Pry?

HOWARD. *(Sighs.)* All right, son—! *(Points sternly at l. arm chair and after waiting for a confused JEFF to cross to and sit on it, closes door.)* Now then ... Irma here has a theory—

IRMA. It's no theory! Barney and me, we witnessed the whole thing! If he ain't chopped the old girl up, where *is* she?

HOWARD. Irma, please! *(Addresses SAM.)* It seems that nobody has seen Amy since I left this place last night. This morning at the brunch, I'm told, you said she was in here resting but—

JEFF. *(Insists.)* Well, she *was,* sheriff!

SCOOTER. *(A warning.)* Jeff—

JEFF. She was! I stopped by later and—

HOWARD. You actually *saw* her here?

JEFF. Not exactly, but—

(He starts to point at SCOOTER.)

SCOOTER. *(Through clenched teeth.)* Jeff!

HOWARD. *(To SCOOTER.)* Wait, little gal, let him have his say. *(To JEFF.)* If you didn't *see* Mrs. Galway, how did you know she was here?

JEFF. Scooter spoke to her.

SCOOTER. *(Quietly.)* Oh boy.

JEFF. *(Can't imagine what he's done wrong.)* Mrs. Galway was in the bathroom!

IRMA. She's *always* in the bathroom! *(Darkly.)* Except when you check—then you find she *ain't!*

HOWARD. Hold on, Irma. *(To JEFF.)* After this young woman spoke to her, did you happen to hear Mrs. Galway answer?

JEFF. *(As SCOOTER holds her breath.)* Well, uh ....

IRMA. *(On her feet.)* You're sworn to tell the truth, young man!

HOWARD. Please!

(IRMA sits.)

JEFF. *(Feeling the pressure.)* The fact is—no, I didn't.

IRMA. Ha!

SAM. *(Starts to rise.)* Howard, I can give you a simple explanation—

HOWARD. *(Interrupts with authority.)* I'd appreciate it, Sam, if *you'd* stay sitting too—and if you don't try laying the same wild story on me you apparently laid on Irma. We checked all the area hospitals and Amy's not in any one of them.

SAM. *(As straightforwardly as he can.)* That isn't necessarily the simple explanation I was about to give.

HOWARD. Good. See, with Barney and Irma calling me in, that makes my visit official—and any explanation you give *now,* simple or not, can be used against you.

SAM. *Huh.*

(SAM exchanges a glance with SCOOTER and shuts his mouth.)

HOWARD. OK, we'll forget the explanation for a minute. The fact is, Amy wasn't here when you led people to believe she was.

IRMA. Or she *was* here—in that trunk!

HOWARD. Irma! *(Continues to SAM.)* I've got tell you, Sam, if you lied this morning, it doesn't really matter. The reason could be as simple as: You and the new bride had a fight, she ran out to cool off a little and you were too embarrassed to let anybody know.

SAM. *(Likes the story, would repeat it.)* As a matter of fact—

IRMA. You're leading the witness!

HOWARD. *(Patience tested.)* This is not a trial!!! *(Mutters darkly.)* Not yet anyway. *(Continuing to IRMA.)* I am merely offering one of the many possible and *innocent* reasons why Sam might have lied to you. Up to that point, whatever happened, it was nobody's business but his and Amy's— *(To SCOOTER.)* and possibly yours, uh—

JEFF. *(As HOWARD hesitates.)* Eileen.

SAM. *(Simultaneously.)* Scooter.

JEFF. Scooter.

SAM. *(Simultaneously.)* Eileen.

HOWARD. Whatever. *(Addresses SAM again.)* But I have to warn you, the picture changed tonight. Barney and Irma Pry, two concerned citizens, took turns watching your doorway. And they observed that not only did Amy not return here, but in the course of the evening there was considerable pounding—the kind that might have come from a hatchet striking some unnamed object—as well as a good deal of cursing and screaming.

SAM. *(Protests.)* But that was *me!* I darn near chopped my arm off!

HOWARD. I warned you about simple explanations—

SAM. It's true, don't you see? *(Shows his bandaged finger.)* And, look, there's blood on the floor—and on the hatchet too!

IRMA. *(Notices it now.)* Ye gods—there *is* blood there!

HOWARD. *(Friend to friend.)* Will you stop it, Sam? You're just digging yourself in deeper.

SAM. *(Rises.)* But I have nothing—almost nothing—to hide! *(Starts in general direction of hatchet.)* Howard, all I did was—

HOWARD. *(Warns, a hand not far from his holster.)* Stay away from that hatchet.

SAM. *(Retreats.)* I'm away! I'm away! Tell them will you, A— Eileen? All I did—

SCOOTER. All he did was try to chop that trunk up, Howard—

the big trunk Jeff brought in last night! And when he couldn't, he had to drag it out.

IRMA. I *told* you we saw him dragging it!

HOWARD. Yeah ... so you did. *(No less suspicious.)* Where did you drag it, Sam?

SAM. Well, I put it in my car—

HOWARD. You have a car down here? Since when?

SAM. I *rented* one. I put the trunk in the back seat and took it to a dump.

IRMA. You rented a whole car just for *that?*

SAM. No, I also had to get a cot because— *(Puts the brakes on.)* Never mind that now. What's important is, I found the dump while I was driving.

HOWARD. Then the trunk's still there?

IRMA. And we can forensically examine it—like they do on Law & Order?

HOWARD. *(Intense.) Can* we, Sam—and thereby rule out any evidence of foul play?

SCOOTER. *(Brightens.)* Why, of course you can!

JEFF. *(Relief.)* I knew this would work out all right.

SCOOTER. *(To SAM.)* Tell him.

SAM. Yeah, well, you *could* examine it, Howard... except I burned it.

SCOOTER. *(Hopes dashed.)* Oh Sam!

IRMA. Get the cuffs on him! He's a maniac!

HOWARD. *(To IRMA.)* Will you stay *out* of this?!

SAM. There was a fire going, see? I had a lot to think about. So I pushed the trunk in and watched it char and smoke and flame away— *(Finishes miserably.)* down to the last splinter.

(SAM sits again, life in ruins.)

HOWARD. *(Sighs.)* Well, I've been reluctant to say this, but with

the blood, the pounding and the screaming and the disappearing trunk,
I've got to ask you at this point ... to produce Amy.

JEFF. *(A technicality.)* But isn't it up to the State, sheriff, to produce her?

HOWARD. Not when there is *prima facie* evidence. We don't need a *dead* body, he has to show us a *live* one. Can you do that, Sam?

SCOOTER. *(Rises.)* Wait! Suppose he *can?* Suppose he says that "live body's" *here*—in this condo, right this minute! Suppose he says she's—

SAM. *(Would stop her.)* Amy—Eileen!

SCOOTER. Yes! Suppose he says she's *me*—Amy Eileen "Scooter" Halloran Galway?! And what if he says I came here last night as an old woman but was intrigued by what I saw printed on Jeff's tee shirt and Ponce de Leon and all!—and after you and Jeff went out, I prayed to a wonderful Irish saint and drank not Coca-Cola but the *real* Real Thing? *Then* what if he says I awoke this morning looking just as I do now—*and* have pictures of myself at nineteen? *Old* pictures that *prove* I'm Amy?

IRMA. *(Shrewd.)* Or you look a little like her because maybe you're related?

SAM, JEFF & SCOOTER. Stay out of this!

SCOOTER. *(Continuing.)* Seriously, Howard, what about that? Suppose that *was* his story—*my* story! *Then* what?

(There is a pregnant pause as all regard HOWARD with mixed hopes.)

HOWARD. *(Turns at last to SAM.)* The question remains—can you produce Amy or can't you?

SCOOTER. *(Seeing she has lost, sits.)* It was worth a try.

JEFF. *(Consoling.)* Sure was.

HOWARD. *(As a disappointed SAM stays silent, yields a long sigh.*) All right, I'm afraid I've gotta ask you and Eileen here to accompany me to headquarters.

SAM. *(Rises, shocked.)* You'd take *her?* Why would you take *her?*

HOWARD. If you're in it, she sure is.

IRMA. They've probably been planning it for years!

SAM. *(Cold determination.)* I'm sorry—but you will *not* take her.

HOWARD. Sam—

SAM. Damn it, Howard, you won't! And the reason you won't is— *(Inspiration.)* Amy's in that bathroom right this minute!

IRMA. Don't let him fool you! He tried that on me.

HOWARD. *(As determined as SAM.)* No one's fooling anyone. What's the game, Sam?

SAM. Who said there was a game? I've spent as much time in court as you have and know a *little* about the law. Suppose I say not only is Amy in the bathroom— *(Looks through open bathroom door.)* I'm looking at her *now?*

HOWARD. *(Weighing his words carefully.)* Naturally I'd want to look too.

SAM. *(Shrewd.)* Want to? You'd have to! Because you know if we ever go to court, I could say Irma was mistaken this morning—Amy was in the bathroom all along—and I *told* you she was, but you wouldn't look. Then even if she never turned up again, your case—which is circumstantial at best—would be laughed out of the building.

HOWARD. *(Sighs.)* All right, you've got me.... I'll look.

(HOWARD starts for door but SAM closes it.)

SAM. Oh? You have a warrant, do you?

HOWARD. *(Tries to disguise his frustration.)* I can get one. You know that.

SAM. Not right away you can't. It's three o'clock in the morning.

HOWARD. I know a judge who's up at the crack of dawn—and as long as I'm already here, I can take you two in for questioning, warrant or not.

SAM. Sure you can. That's because I tacitly allowed you entrance to my home. But that doesn't go for the bathroom. No sir. You'll need a warrant for that.

HOWARD. Look, if you're going to get tough about it—

(HOWARD reaches for his handcuffs.)

SAM. *(Grins.)* Not me. I believe I've made my point. *(Opens bathroom door.)* See? She isn't in there anyhow.

HOWARD. *(Glances about in bathroom, a hand still on his cuffs.)* What in tarnation are you up to?

JEFF. *(An aside to SCOOTER.)* This is fascinating, do you know that?

SAM. *(Continues to HOWARD.)* I'll tell you in a minute. But first, why don't we get started for headquarters?

HOWARD. *(Beyond frustration.)* Whatever you're trying to pull—

SAM. *(All innocence.)* Howard, I'm volunteering to go with you! Do you want me to go or not?

SCOOTER. *(An excited aside to SAM as HOWARD stands baffled.)* What *are* we trying to pull?

SAM. *(Aside to SCOOTER.)* Just keep trusting me, will you? *(Louder.)* Come on, Irma. You too, Jeff. Let's go.

HOWARD. *(At last releases handcuffs.)* All right. We'll *all* go down to headquarters.

IRMA. *(Aside to HOWARD.)* He's still trying to fool you. Watch him!

HOWARD. *(Explodes.)* I'm watching him, woman! What more do you want me to *do?*

SAM. *(At door, to IRMA.)* After you, my dear.

IRMA. You won't be so smart, big boy, when they start squirting you with those rubber hoses.

(IRMA exits.)

JEFF. *(Quietly.)* I sure hope it works, Mr. Galway, whatever it is.

(JEFF follows IRMA off.)

SAM. *(To SCOOTER.)* You're next, Eileen. Come on. *(She reluctantly starts out.)* Oh! The kitchen light....

SCOOTER. *(Changes direction for the kitchen.)* I'll get it.

HOWARD. Sam, I know you think you've established some fine legal point—

SAM. *(Super confident.)* And I *have,* Howard. Come a little closer, I'll tell you what it is. *(As HOWARD reluctantly approaches.)* You understand—I didn't want to say this in front of Irma, but .... *(As HOWARD leans in close to SAM and therefore the door, SAM shoves it with all his might, propelling HOWARD almost totally outside.)* Good *night,* Howard!

HOWARD. *(Pushing back.)* Sam!

SAM. *(Grunting as he works.)* I know you hate to leave, but—! *(With SCOOTER rushing over to help, the two manage to get the door slammed)* you're out of here!

HOWARD. *(Off, a wounded shout.)* What in tarnation are you doing?

SCOOTER. *(Thrilling.)* What in tarnation did we *do?*

SAM. *(Shouts through door.)* We established you don't have a warrant, you dumb Milwaukee flatfoot! *(To SCOOTER, giddy.)* He doesn't have a warrant!

IRMA. *(Off.)* Break it down! Break that door down!

SAM. *(Calls off.)* You've don't even have a good circumstantial case! No body, no weapon, nothing! Come in this door and any hope of a successful prosecution goes right out the window! In the door, out the window! Do you read me?

HOWARD. *(Off, sheer frustration.)* Dang it, Sam!...

SAM. *Do you read me, Howard?*

HOWARD. *(Off.)* All right, I'll *get* a warrant! But I'm deputizing Irma—do you read *me?* And I'm giving her my gun!

IRMA. *(Off.)* I know how to use it too. You'd better believe I do!

HOWARD. *(Off.)* Set one foot outside before I get back, Sam Galway—

SAM. *(That giddiness again.)* Not me! There's a copperhead out there!

HOWARD. *(Off, farther away.)* I'll be back. Count on it.

SAM. I'll be here!

IRMA. *(Off.)* I'll be here too!

JEFF. *(Off.)* Scooter?... I'll be here too.

SCOOTER. *(Kind of loves that boy.)* I know, Jeff! I know!

(SAM and SCOOTER move away from door.)

SAM. *(Coming down from the high, an apologetic laugh.)* Ha! I'm sorry, hon—but when he said he was going to take *you....*

SCOOTER. *(Embraces him.)* Oh sweetheart! *Don't* be sorry! This day of mine—it just keeps getting better and better! *(A pause, pulls back from him, their arms still around each other.)* But what do we do *now?*

SAM. *(His eyes impacting hers.)* Scoot, I guess we do everything in our power—to produce Aunt Amy.

(Her eyes return the impact; she nods to show her trust and there is a blackout on the scene.)

Scene 3

(In the blackout, a rooster crows.)

SAM. *(Who is as yet unseen.)* Well, we tried. *(A match flares as SAM lights a pipe, lights rising partially on the next morning; he is dressed in his robe and pajamas and sits at foot of bed; SAM's WIFE, who lies swathed in a sheet and blanket, does not move.)* ... Didn't we, hon?

SAM'S WIFE. *(Who still sounds a lot like SCOOTER, sleepily.)* Huh.

SAM. *(A thought.)* You ... uh ... don't *feel* any different, do you?

SAM'S WIFE. Huh.

SAM. *(Hopeful.) Do* you?

SAM'S WIFE. Uh.

SAM. *(The realist.)* That's what I thought. *(He just sits smoking for a moment before he adds:)* It sure was worth a try though.

SAM'S WIFE. Yes, Sam. It was!

SAM. Whatever happens now, I'm glad about one thing. See, all day yesterday I kept blaming *you,* thinking that the trouble was you were so darned young! But now I see I should have been blaming *me*—because the *real* trouble was ... I was so darned old!

SAM'S WIFE. But you weren't, Sam! You *aren't!*

SAM. I *was,* the way I saw it. I just didn't have the strength to keep up with you and—more than anything else, I guess—that's the thing that scared me. But then, when we threw Howard out *(Smiles at the memory.)* Mmmm!—well, I knew it wasn't strength I needed. What I needed was what every one on this sorrowful, wonderful planet of ours seems to need. Young or old, it makes no difference. I needed courage—and just didn't have it.

SAM'S WIFE. But you did, Sam! You had it when it counted. That means you had it all along!

SAM. Well, I don't think I'll be so scared anymore. That's

something.

SAM'S WIFE. It's *everything.*

SAM. *(Muses.) Almost* everything—yeah. *(Rises to stretch; there is a knock on the door; surprised:)* Can that be Howard? He's never this prompt!

HOWARD. *(Off.)* Sam! I've got the warrant!

SAM. *(Sighs.)* Until today.

(SAM starts for door.)

SAM'S WIFE. *(Surprised.)* You're not going to let him in?

SAM. How can I keep him out? Listen, if you're worried about being taken to the station—

SAM'S WIFE. *(Gathers up bedclothes.)* Not like *this* I'm not being taken to the station! Stall him!

(SAM's WIFE hurries into bathroom, closing door—the dimness and the sheet and blanket having prevented us from seeing her clearly; SAM goes to wall switch and clicks it on—lights rising to full.)

HOWARD. *(Off.)* Sam!

IRMA. *(Off.)* Are you going to break that door down or not?

HOWARD. *(Off.)* There's two ways I can come in, Sam—through this door or *through* it.

SAM. All right! I'll get it open.

(With a glance toward bathroom to make sure the door is closed, SAM opens porch door and we see HOWARD with IRMA just behind him.)

HOWARD. *(Extends the warrant, the cool professional.)* This permits me entry, search and the power to arrest you both. Care to examine it?

SAM. *(Takes the finely printed legal document and, after a squinting attempt to read it, hands it back.)* I'll take your word for it.

(Sam steps back to permit HOWARD and IRMA to enter.)

HOWARD. *(Looking about.)* Where's Eileen?

IRMA. Don't tell me he's done away with her too!

SAM. Sorry to disappoint you. She just stepped out.

HOWARD. *(Aware of the rumpled bed, shakes his head.)* At your age, Sam. At your age.

SAM. *(Wrists extended.)* Going to put the cuffs on me?

HOWARD. Going to give me any more trouble?

SAM. … No.

HOWARD. No trouble, no cuffs. *(Having checked other likely places, raps on bathroom door.)* Miss, you in there? Let's go, it's the sheriff.

SAM'S WIFE. *(Off.)* Let me see the color of your warrant!

HOWARD. But Sam already— *(Looks at SAM, who shrugs.)* All right. *(Slips it under door and addresses SAM.)* Someday, you know, you're going to have to explain this whole dang thing to me—and I'll either die laughing or crying. *(Raps on door again.)* Well? Is everything in order?

SAM'S WIFE. *(Off, begins to laugh.)* It—it seems to be.

HOWARD. What's so funny?

SAM'S WIFE. *(Continues to laugh.)* Oh my! Oh my!

SAM. *(Concerned, calls in through door.)* What is it, hon?

IRMA. *(To HOWARD.)* It's some kind of trick. Be careful!

SAM. Are you all right? What's going on?

SAM'S WIFE. *(Off, still laughing.)* I'm all right! I'm fine! In fact, I'm just—wonderful! *(Throws door open and enters fully dressed, warrant in hand.)* And I can't read a thing without my glasses!

(HOWARD and IRMA react in shock and confusion and SAM in warm surprise—for she is the AMY we first knew.)

HOWARD. *(Gasps.)* Amy! Mrs. Galway!

SAM. *(Embraces her.)* Sweetheart!

IRMA. This is *her?* This is Amy? Where's the other one?

HOWARD. Yeah! How—

SAM. Don't you get it, Howard? Don't you finally see the picture? She's been here all along.

HOWARD. *(How could he be so stupid?)* The shower curtain! I never thought to look behind it!

IRMA. I looked behind it yesterday! And there was no one there! *(Exits into bathroom, continuing off.)* See for yourself! No one is there *now!*

SAM. *(Confidential to HOWARD.)* Just how much trust do you think you can place in a witness like Irma? I'll be she never even saw Scooter leave.

IRMA. *(Reentering.)* She *didn't!* She *never* left—not alive at least! *(As she visually checks kitchen:)* Barney will swear to it, same as me!

(JEFF enters as IRMA turns away from kitchen.)

IRMA. And so will *Jeff!* He watched with us all night!

JEFF. *(Not seeing AMY yet.)* Swear to what? What's going on?

HOWARD. Irma says you're willing to swear you never saw Eileen leave. Are you? Come on, Jeff. Your eyes are a little younger than hers and Barney's.

IRMA. You're darn fine tootin' they are! *(To JEFF.)* Tell him, kid. Then there'll be no doubt about it.

JEFF. *(Now sees AMY and reacts, eyes fixed on her.)* Oh! Well! The trouble is ... I think I *did* kind of see her leave. Yeah, she said she'd have to, very, very suddenly, and never, never be able to come back. And I think I kind of saw that. Yeah.

IRMA. *(At wit's end.)* Pay no attention to him! He's gone crazy! *Everybody's* gone crazy!

JEFF. You might be right, Mrs. Pry. Then again.... *(Another look at AMY.)* It's awful nice to see you again, Mrs. Galway.

AMY. *(Touches his arm, making it clear they have reached some sort of understanding.)* It's nice to see *you.*

JEFF. I know I'll miss Scooter.

AMY. She misses you already.

JEFF. *(Unable to take it any longer.)* Well...! *(Turns to SAM.)* You're a very lucky man, Mr. Galway.

(JEFF exits.)

IRMA. Will you *stop* that boy?! He perjured himself! I'm telling you she never left! Me and Barney, we never took our eyes off this place!

HOWARD. Why is it, Irma, I somehow have trouble believing that?

(He begins to lead her to the door.)

IRMA. *(Protests.)* But we watched this place all night! Watched the door! Watched the windows! Will you stop shoving me? Nobody entered! Nobody left! Will you stop it with the shoving? *(Poised in the doorway.)* Barney! Tell this crazy person— Damn it, Barney! Are you asleep again?

(IRMA exits, HOWARD looking after her a moment before he turns to SAM and AMY.)

HOWARD. Folks, while I regret the mix-up and all the accusations ... I'd appreciate it next time if you two could be just a little more straightforward with me.

AMY. We'll be as straightforward as you like, Howard—*if* you'll believe our story.

HOWARD. Well, if it isn't as wild as the last one you gave me— I mean, all that stuff about some Irish saint and Ponce de Leon—!

AMY. But *I* never gave you that story—Scooter did.

HOWARD. *(Thrown.)* But didn't you say—I mean, didn't *she* say— *(Stops as he realizes how confused he is.)* They'll be starting the brunch early. I hope they're serving drinks.

(HOWARD exits, closing door.)

SAM. *(Goes to her.)* Amy!...

AMY. *(Neatly sidesteps him to get her purse.)* Not now, Sam! There's a recipe I have to jot down for Jeff's mother—and a note I have to write. *(Puts glasses on and notices:)* And you've got to put some *clothes* on!

SAM. *(A better idea in mind.)* Do we *have* to go to the brunch today?

AMY. It's for Aunt Amy! Poor dear—she couldn't make the last one!

SAM. *(Game.)* See you in a second. *(Finds his clothes and takes them into bathroom; she has meanwhile found a pen and paper in her purse and started writing; off:)* It's funny, Amy—you know? When you left the room just now, I could have sworn you were still Scooter.

AMY. *(Busy.)* I thought so myself! But I don't see how that's possible! We'd already duplicated all of the conditions.

SAM. *(Off.)* Did we? All of them?

AMY. I know I said an awful lot of prayers to St. Dymphna.

SAM. *(Off.)* Sure, asking her to help you grow up a little.

AMY. Either that or— *(Stops writing as another thought occurs to her.)* Oh oh.

SAM. *(Off.)* What is it, pet?

AMY. *(Comes to her feet.)* You didn't happen to, uh—drink any of the tap water just now—did you?

SAM. *(Off.)* A drop or two, maybe—I'm brushing my teeth!

AMY. *(Concern.)* I'm not sure that's such a good idea. See, it occurs to me that drinking the water was the one thing we *didn't* duplicate—not till this morning when I brushed *my* teeth.

SAM. *(Off.)* ... So?

AMY. Don't you understand? I kept praying to St. Dymphna that she'd help me return from the age when I was so desperately in love—but when *that* didn't seem to work....

SAM. *(Off, encouraging.)* ... Yeah?

AMY. *(Almost afraid to tell him.)* I said a *second* prayer, that's all.

SAM. *(Off.)* What do you mean, you said a second prayer? What are you talking about?

AMY. *(Opens bathroom door a crack to peek in and, with her worst fears realized, low key:)* Geemanetly.

SAM. *(Off.)* What is it? What's the problem?

AMY. *(Her heart going out to him.)* I don't know for sure—but whatever it is—I think we're going to be the hit of the brunch again!

(AMY'S HUSBAND enters puzzled; he still wears a super-large bandage on his finger and has donned the clothes we saw him in yesterday; but they no longer fit as well; in fact, there is room for a volleyball in the waistband and the pants drag on the floor; all this is probably due to the fact that he is now fourteen years old; AMY sighs, smiles and takes his arm; and as the two start off together, lights fall on the final act of "AMY'S WISH.")

PRODUCTION NOTES

Regarding St. Dymphna: There really is an Irish saint by that name and though she is not usually considered the patron saint of brides, the story of her life and martyrdom is such that it seems a fitting tribute to her. As to the idea of her fulfilling a bride's wedding night prayer—or wish—we can blame Amy's mother for this happy fiction.

Regarding all the water Sam drinks in Act I, Scene 3: We must be kind to our leading men. So at rise he is finishing half a glass or less. When he pours some from the pitcher, he may pour and start to drink it with his back to us so we do not know he has, in fact, poured very little. When he takes the pitcher d.c. and drinks it all, this is readily accomplished if the pitcher is opaque and almost empty—but it can also be accomplished with the kind of pitcher available in magic shops and on the Internet. They are transparent and can seem to be quite full while holding very little. With that very little "poured," they are revealed as quite empty.

Regarding Sam's reference to the Rolling Stones: times change, and when they do, it is recommended that the name be changed to that of another aging, active rock group that has been around a long, long time.

Regarding exactly when the "real" Amy is reintroduced: it is recommended that Act II, Scene 3 be begun with the actress who plays Scooter, her voice continuing off, and the actual switch not occur until Sam's wife's final o.s. line: "In fact, I'm just—wonderful!," Scooter saying, "In fact, I'm just— "and Amy saying "wonderful!" just before she enters with: "And I can't read a thing without my glasses!"

Regarding the 14-year-old Sam: Since he has no lines or business except for his climactic entrance, it is recommended that he is *not* listed in the program and thereby kept as a surprise.

PROPERTY LIST

<u>ACT I</u>

<u>Scene 1</u>

Preset:
Sheets and blanket on bed
Pillows, towels, washcloth and shampoo in closet
Three suitcases (one jonquil) brought in with two raincoats during
first brief blackout.

Carried on by:
JEFF:
     Two suitcases
     Wooden trunk containing two blouses, blue jeans and hatchet
     Ballpoint pen
SAM:
     Notebook
     Glass of water
AMY:
     Large purse that holds glasses, compact, pen and paper
HOWARD:
     Big black umbrella

<u>Scene 2</u>

Carried on by:
SAM:
     Tie
     Newspaper
IRMA:
     Small, colorful umbrella
     Empty pack of Camels

AMY:

Damp washcloth

Scene 3

Preset:

Suitcases

Various books and tools, including hatchet

Water pitcher, newspaper and compact

Scrapbook

Carried on by:

SAM:

Partially filled water glass

JEFF:

Box of candy

IRMA:

Soup tureen

ACT II

Scene 1

Preset:

Bed (converted from sofa)

A small amount of red liquid on floor

Strike:

Trunk, suitcases, books and tools

Water pitcher, glass, newspaper and compact

Scrapbook

Carried on by:
AMY:
    Two coffee mugs
SAM:
    Folding cot and hatchet
    Big bandage (worn on finger)
HOWARD:
    Handkerchief

Scene 2

Carried on by:
JEFF:
    Small drill

Scene 3

Preset:
Pipe, tobacco, wooden matches
Ashtray

Strike:
Red liquid
Coffee mugs

Carried on by:
HOWARD:
    Warrant
YOUNG SAM:
    Big bandage (worn on finger)

SOUND EFFECTS

ACT I

Scene 1

Organ music—including final 15 notes of Lohengrin Wedding March
Rain
Lightning and thunder

Scene 2

Loud alarm
Rooster crow
TV sound (preferably a brief sound bite from a soap opera theme)

Scene 3

Rooster crow

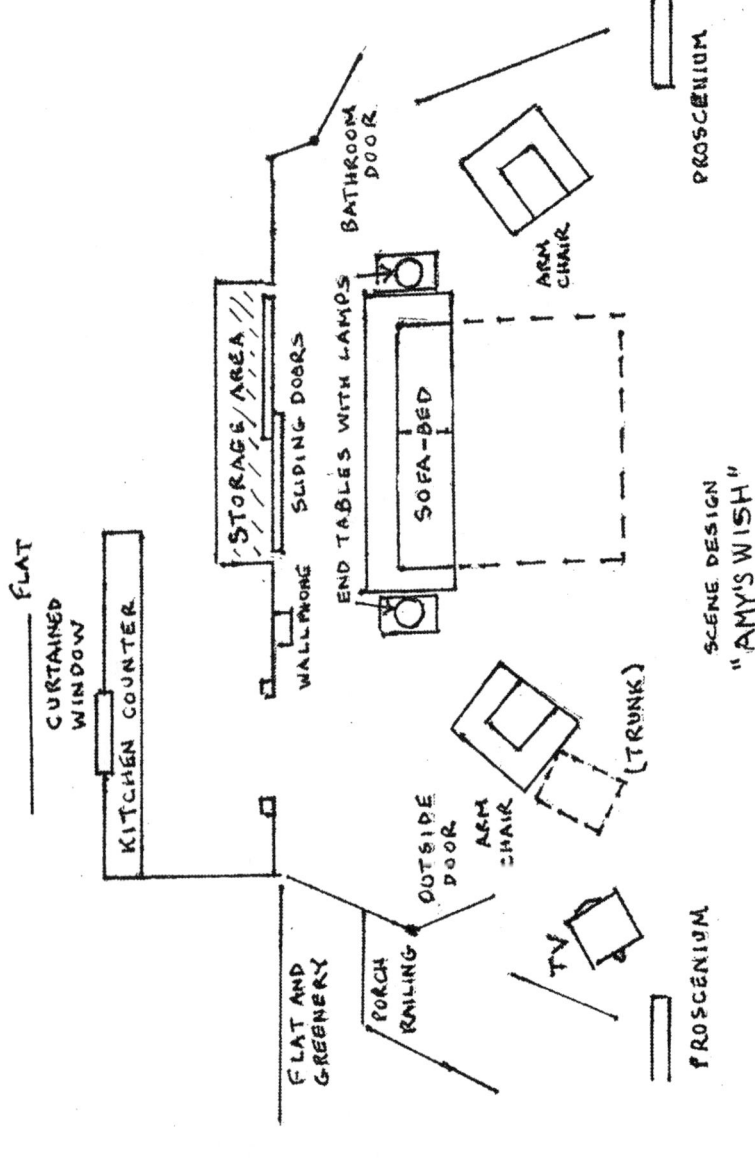

FLAT

CURTAINED WINDOW

KITCHEN COUNTER

STORAGE AREA

SLIDING DOORS

WALLPHONE

END TABLES WITH LAMPS

BATHROOM DOOR

SOFA-BED

ARM CHAIR

ARM CHAIR

(TRUNK)

OUTSIDE DOOR

TV

PORCH RAILING

FLAT AND GREENERY

PROSCENIUM

PROSCENIUM

SCENE DESIGN
"AMY'S WISH"

Flight
ARTHUR GIRON

"A witty, touching flashback…There is poignancy
between the laughs." —*The New York Times*

The author doesn't claim it happened exactly this way. He has taken
real-life characters and biographical information and supposed what
it was like for Orville and Wilbur growing up in the dysfunctional
Wright family. They are portrayed as boys whose mischief is just a
sign of frustrated brilliance. Not a documentary, the play explores
the dynamics of the Wright family in theatrical terms. 4 m., 1 f.
(#8179)

Pride's Crossing
TINA HOWE

Best American Play of 1998
New York Drama Critics Circle

"A play you will remember and forever cherish.…It is rich in both
texture and imagination."— *New York Post*
"A lovely achievement…Mabel becomes a woman who … both
typified her time and her class and transcended it."—*Variety*

At ninety, Mabel Tidings Bigelow insists on celebrating her daughter and granddaughter's annual visit with a croquet party. As the
party unfolds, she relives vignettes from the past that reveal the pre-
cise moment of opportunity lost and love rejected that define her
life. The vibrant portrait of Mabel that takes shape culminates in her
one shining achievement when she became the first woman to swim
the English Channel. 4 m., 3 f. (#18230)

Send for your copy of the Samuel French
BASIC CATALOGUE OF PLAYS AND MUSICALS

The Blue Room
Adapted by DAVID HARE
From *La Ronde* by Arthur Schnitzler

"The hottest show in town."—*New York Post*

"Generates enough erotic energy to raise the dead…. A funny, intelligent and razor-sharp satire."—*New York Daily News*

"A range-stretching exercise for actors."—*The New York Times*

A sensation in New York and London, *The Blue Room* depicts a daisy chain of ten encounters between five women and five men; all portrayed by a single actor and actress. Each couple is seen before and after having sex; then one moves on to another partner. 1 m., 1 f. (#4275)

Amy's View
DAVID HARE

"Funny, moving, difficult, fascinating. A major dramatist has written a strong, rich play."— *The London Times*

"Above all else, *Amy's View* offers the sheer exhilaration of watching a major dramatist writing for the theatre he loves at the very height of his powers."—*London Daily Express*

After sold-out performances at the National Theatre prompted a transfer to the West End, Judi Dench came to Broadway to star in this heady and original drama of love and death. Esme Allen is a well-known British actress caught in a changing theatrical climate. A visit from her daughter with her new boyfriend sets in motion events which gel sixteen years later. 3 m., 3 f. (#3709)

David Hare was honored with a special citation from the New York Drama Critics for contributions, including *The Blue Room* and *Amy's View,* to the New York season.

Send for your copy of the Samuel French BASIC CATALOGUE OF PLAYS AND MUSICALS